THE
DUTCH MOTOR-BARGE
BOOK

The motorizing of the Dutch and Belgian barge fleet 1900-1950

Published by David Evershed Publications,
89 Atlantic Way, Porthtowan,
Truro, Cornwall,
TR4 8AH, England.

ISBN 0953223116

9 780953 223114 >

Booths Printers and Binders, Mabe, Cornwall. 01326 373226

CONTENTS

Front cover.......Luxemotor "*Vertrouwen*".
Back cover.......Brons petrol engine from 1905.

INTRODUCTION

This is a book about motor-barges and the motorizing of the existing sailing-barge fleet of the Netherlands and Belgium in the early and middle part of this century. This era of change was a fascinating time, a time when steam, diesel, petrol, horse-drawn, self-propelled and sail-driven ships could all be found in a single harbour at the same time. The propulsion system of today's motor-barge has its roots firmly in the nineteenth century and owes much to steam engine technology. The late industrial revolution, market forces and two world wars, all played their part in propelling the commercial barge and its propulsion system firmly into the twentieth century, into the high performance, enormous load carrying, high-tech monsters of today. Many skippers resisted change and so too did shipbuilders, slowly but surely they were left behind. Many however felt that they knew when a fine balance had been struck. They knew when to stop, and today, on most of the major waterways of the Netherlands and Belgium, you will still find ships that are virtually unchanged from the time between the wars. These are the luxemotors, spitsen, motortjalken and beurtschepen that found a particular niche for themselves and where that need still exists, so too do the ships. A good many of the smaller ships still trading, are ex-sailing-barges that managed to change with the times and stay competitive. At least half of the private, motorized, barges in Europe and England are ex-sailing-barges. Because of this I have also detailed how the different types of sailing-barges took to the adaptation to power. This in itself is a fascinating story that runs in harmony with the development of the pure motor-ship. Steam played a great part in the genesis of the motor-barge. Steam tugs were the first motor-ships on the inland waters of the Netherlands. The lessons learnt here, with regard to an efficient screw propeller system and a good hull shape, were later embraced by their petrol and oil burning successors.

This is a book for barge enthusiasts, addressing an area that has sadly been neglected, not least because of the translation problems involved! In this area I am once again indebted to my wife Margreet, without whose patience and editing skills I would still be lost in my dictionary. Today a new breed of barge owners has evolved, those of us who live on board and sail our ships for pleasure rather than any monetary reward. For this happy band of skippers and would-be barge owners, I have included chapters on original construction techniques, designed purpose, possible pitfalls inherent in some conversions and, for what it is worth, some of my practical experiences of living on and skippering, both motorized sailing-barges and purpose-built motor-barges.

For the linguistically challenged, and as far as the Dutch language is concerned that is no disgrace believe me, I have compiled a glossary of Dutch barge terms that appear in the text and also words that you may encounter when sorting through the paperwork associated with buying and owning a barge. A section on original registration numbers and what they mean, will be of interest to those researching the history of their own barge.

Finally, a big thank you to everyone who has made this book possible, there are too many to name all of you, but you know who you are, and once again thanks for answering my questions and letting me poke about in the most distant recesses of your ships!

David Evershed, *"Jan Willem"*, Falmouth. July 1998.

David is an experienced barge skipper and has logged many miles on both sail and motor powered barges. He lives with his Dutch born wife Margreet on board their zeiltjalk "Jan Willem" in Cornwall.

1) The motor-barge "*Hester*" displays many original features, along with some necessary alterations, designed to keep her competitive.

2) Deutz, deck mounted diesel engine, powering the deck equipment on "*Hester*".

CHAPTER ONE

External and internal combustion engines

I know that this is a book about barges and not specifically the history of engines, but since here we are particularly interested in motor-barges, I am assuming that you, the reader, will also have an interest in the many, growling, hissing, beasts that have been used to drive the ships.

As I said in my introduction, the shape of the motor-barge and its motive power is inextricably linked to the evolution of the steam engine. In the later stages of the nineteenth century, steam had been driving engines of various sorts for several hundred years. Evolving from early, inefficient, highly dangerous machines, to surprisingly reliable (though strictly speaking still hideously inefficient), dangerous machines. Once the process of setting a steam engine in motion is initiated, from the early stoking of the furnace right through to the final dying wisps of steam, it must be constantly attended. Failure to do so is dealt with harshly. Either the machine just does not run, or worse still it blows up and kills you. There was obviously room for improvement and all over Europe men were searching for the answer. The full story is long, complicated and very interesting, however here we will stick to the major players in the drama that culminated in the engines we know today.

It was the Dutchman, Huygens, in the 17th century, who first had a go at building an internal combustion engine. He based his logic on that of the recoil that occurs when a cannon is fired. He therefore used gunpowder as his fuel. Very basically his engine involved a piston, a cylinder, a small amount of black powder and a lighted match. It was not a resounding success. In the seventeenth century the way forward, towards the industrial revolution, was the steam engine, which of course is an external combustion engine (the combustion is not taking place inside a sealed chamber). The standard engine of the day in England was the Newcomen steam engine, widely used as a pumping engine for mines. It ran at 10 rpm and used 13 tons of coal a day. It was both fuel and thermally inefficient, but it was all there was. The eighteenth century saw James Watt take a stab at the problem and by separating the condensing and steam injection sides of the engine, he at once produced a more fuel economic engine and more importantly, one that was double acting. That is to say that both strokes of the piston produced power. His engines were also much smaller than the Newcomen units and so they found a home in mills and industry. Now we come to the nineteenth century and the industrial revolution proper. In Cornwall, in the tin mining areas of the far south west of England, Trevithick developed the high pressure steam engine. These were lighter, simpler, more powerful, faster and crucially more reliable. Trevithick was the first man to build a self-propelled steam engine. His engines moved out of the factory and into the countryside in the form of motorized ploughing and threshing machines and, for the first time, on to the water, where they powered dredging machines. Now the steam engine really took off. The first steamboat crossed the Atlantic as early as 1819. By 1840 Stephenson type locomotives snorted their way along steel rails all over Europe and beyond and by 1865 the first double expansion engine, the compound engine arrived. The availability of steel as a manufacturing material, as opposed to iron, meant that stronger boilers, able to take higher compression forces, were built. Steel boilers and double, then triple expansion, increased efficiency by allowing the expanding steam to expand even farther, in separate cylinders, to increase power and efficiency.

3) The DAF 475 (van **D**oorne's **A**utomobiel **F**abriek),in the authors ship, the zeiltjalk "*Jan Willem*". The cylinder head has been removed for servicing. Note the cunning use of the mainsheet tackle to handle the heavy cylinder head. The engine is located under the cockpit, in the space formerly occupied by the skipper's double bunk.

Within 20 years triple expansion engines were common and it is in this form that the steam engine successfully powered boats right up until late in the twentieth century.

The steam engine is crucial in the development of the true internal combustion engine. All of the early research utilized much of the known engineering knowledge accumulated from the reciprocating piston steam engine. The late 19th century was a fast breeding ground for technology. As early as 1860, in France, Lenoir had built an internal combustion engine that ran on coal-gas and air. It was a double-acting two-stroke engine, based on steam design. They were popular in industry, but relying on piped coal-gas, they could not become truly mobile. In Germany, Otto had discovered that by compressing a fuel-air mixture, more powerful combustion was achieved. He worked with his ideas to produce his first four-stroke engine, the extra stroke being the compression stroke. The first Otto four-stroke engine, with spark ignition, ran in 1877. He used a petrol-air mix for a fuel and so, with a petrol tank attached to his motor, it became a reliable, self-propelled unit, much smaller than a steam engine and without the problems of constant attention that a steam engine needed. The internal combustion engine had arrived and was not going to go away. Even today the four-stroke cycle is also known as the Otto cycle. It was still far from perfect however and many brains in many countries set to work on improving it. In England, Herbert Ackroyd Stuart developed a four-stroke engine that ran on oil, rather than gas or petrol. He did not use a spark to ignite the mixture, nor did he exploit high compression to invoke ignition. On the Stuart engine, a "bulb" attached to the combustion chamber was warmed by means of a blowtorch flame applied externally. When this was heated to cherry red and the engine turned over, the combustion space was hot enough to ignite the mixture. The heat of the combustion maintained the heat in the combustion chamber and so on the next cycle the mixture would once again ignite. So, Stuart had a four-stroke, oil burning engine, with no need for troublesome electric spark ignition systems. His motor was popular and found favour in agricultural applications. In the twentieth century, engine makers such as Bolinder and Seffle exploited a similar technique with their own hot bulb engines. This type of engine is usually referred to as a "semi-diesel", or in the Netherlands, a "gloeikop" (glowhead) motor. Meanwhile, at the same time as Otto, Stuart and others were labouring away, a German by the name of Rudolph Diesel had set about starting a revolution of his own.

Rudolph Diesel

As we have seen, in 1860 the Frenchman, Jean Joseph Etienne Lenoir patented the design for an internal combustion engine, running on a mixture of coal-gas and air. Around the same time, Nicholas Otto, after several false starts caused by destruction of his engines due to the higher forces involved in his high compression engine, developed his famous spark ignition, single-acting, four cycle, or four-stroke engine. One stroke for power and three strokes for inlet, compression and exhaust, didn't seem a very good investment initially, but the relatively high power produced easily outweighed all this. Over 8000 of his engines were sold. Where could high compression four-stroke engines go from here?

In France, Rudolph Diesel was also exploring new ideas. Whilst at university he had become aquainted with the ideas of Sadi Carnot regarding the "ideal heat engine". Essentially this was the concept of an engine that had perfect thermal efficiency, lost none of its created energy and crucially would run backwards as well as forwards without any loss in efficiency. In other words it would take a cold medium and convert it to a hot medium (the engine as we know it), or take a hot medium and convert it to cold (a refrigeration plant works this way).

4) Hans, the skipper of the 1950's Spits "*Vasco*", displays his General Motors 270 hp engine, originally intended for a Sherman tank.

5) This Kromhout 4GSV, four-cylinder diesel engine, is one of the first generation of compact, "modern", marine diesel engines. Built in 1954 and with 80 hp available, the optimum power is delivered at 2000 rpm. This shows the engines intended role in the automotive industry.

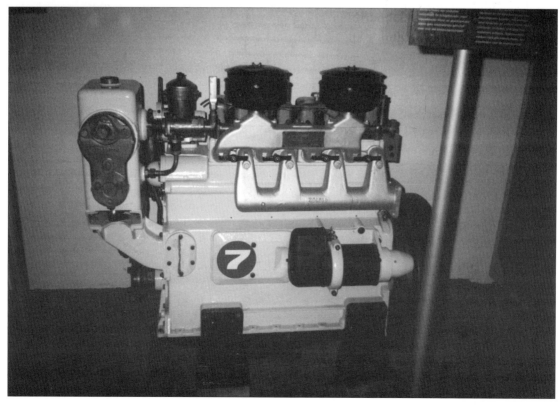

Diesel later spent time working in a refrigeration plant and it is natural that his thoughts first evolved from this area. After he finished his studies he moved back to Germany and embarked upon his quest. His first engines were to run on ammonia, as did the refrigeration units. He got greatly carried away by his ideas and lodged a patent long before his ideas were really practical. For example, he mentions a compression of over 3500 psi when conventional engineering was only achieving around 250 psi. However some people had faith in him and after greatly revising his early specifications, the Machinen Fabrik Augsburg Nurnburg, the MAN engineering company, gave him the chance to build an engine.

Like Otto, he had settled on a four-stroke, single-action cycle, using a compression stroke to create more power. Where his ideas differed though was in the scale of the compression. By taking compression to around 16-1 or higher, the air in the cylinder became hot enough to ignite a fuel source when introduced directly into the combustion chamber. In other words it would burn without any need to ignite it by secondary means. It was a compression ignition engine. In 1894, Diesel's first compression ignition engine ran. It achieved the tremendous compression pressure of 500 psi and was a single-cylinder engine with fuel injection. He had hoped to use the cheapest oil available, but in his first engines he made do with the relatively cheap lamp oil, which was close to what we know as paraffin today. His second engine, in 1895, produced 23 hp and had a thermal efficiency of 26%. A long way from the 100% efficiency of Carnot's ideal heat engine, but it was still a whopping 50% better than a petrol engine and a staggering 100% better than the best steam engine. The fuel was the cruder, cheaper form of petrol called gasoil, that he had hoped to use originally. Today this fuel is almost universally called Diesel oil. His motor clearly had promise. He sold the production rights to MAN and subsequent MAN Diesel engines became better and better and most crucially smaller. The biggest problem however was that of fuel injection. Because of the high compression ratios, a conventional carburetor would never work. The charge of fuel had to be forced into the combustion space at exactly the right moment and at the right pressure, otherwise it would simply be blown straight back out again. These first engines used an externally mounted, crankshaft-driven, compressor, to allow a measured charge of oil to be injected by a blast of high pressure air. It was not until 1920 that the Karl Benz motor company came up with a mechanical injection system, thus eliminating the need for a compressor. This was the first of the "modern" Diesel engines. Ironically, although the compressor was no longer needed for fuel injection purposes, many manufacturers had used the presence of compressed air to develop a compressed air starting system. Many engines therefore retained the compressor purely for starting.

Petroleum versus heavy oil

The Diesel engine was fast becoming a force to be reckoned with in the first part of this century. However, we must not forget that side by side with the development of the "diesel fuel", or "heavy oil" burning compression ignition engine, went the more popular spark ignition engine running on petrol. As far as the engines fitted to most barges go, the vast majority came as a spin-off from other applications. Some manufactures primarily designed for the smaller marine market, but they were few and far between. At sea, steam was still the prime mover and it showed its future potential in the form of "*Turbinia*", the first steam turbine engined boat which "gatecrashed" the Spithead review of 1897, showing off its 34 knot top speed. Faster than any of the Navy boats of the time.

6) Gardner 6LX engine in the luxemotor "*Vertrouwen*". This engine was installed in 1969 replacing the original Brons unit.

7) This vertical, single-cylinder engine by Brons, ran on paraffin. It was available in 1905 and produced 24 hp at 350 rpm. Jan Brons was one of the founding fathers of the Dutch marine diesel industry.

Fast as this was, the man in the street wanted an engine that he could walk up to, start, use and turn off again as often as he liked. Steam was not for him.

In Europe, specialized motor-ships were being built (see *beurtschepen*, chapter 8), using the most freely available diesel engines of the day. The two main contenders here were the Liggende Rennes, a single-cylinder engine with a horizontal rather than vertical configuration and the Brons single-cylinder engine. The Brons was popular in the Netherlands, but being a vertical rather than horizontal design it needed a tall engine-room to house it.

Meanwhile, in England, the Royal Navy had also uncharacteristically recognized the worth of the new technological innovations and had ordered a petrol engined motor torpedo boat from Yarrow Napier. The instruction manual of the day stresses the need for constant attention to lubrication and cooling, along with the importance of keeping the spark ignition system scrupulously dry. It is this last factor, along with the potentially explosive nature of petroleum, that has always rendered the petrol engine less attractive in a marine application. Despite this, it is true that more development work had gone into the petrol engine than the diesel, at least in the early years. The English barge skippers in common with their Dutch colleagues saw the potential in the smaller petrol engines. In 1901 the first recorded instance of a petrol auxiliary engine being installed in a Thames barge occurred, whilst in 1907 the coasting barge "*Arctic*" was converted to a full motor-barge.

The American petrol engine that was used in the car that took the land speed record in 1905, was a 24 litre monster of V8 configuration. This engineering example was built when the Brons single-cylinder diesel was the "state of the art" in Holland. By 1910, Henry Ford was mass producing his model T Ford, an in line four-cylinder petrol engine, and this too found favour in the Netherlands to power "opduwers" (see chapter 3). America loved the petrol engine; they had masses of cheap fuel and so the engines they produced got bigger and thirstier. The 1915 Caddilac had a V8 engine of 5 litres capacity and managed to achieve 65 mph at 12 mpg.

The first world war brought good news to those British barges engaged in shipping coal and coke to France and several acquired auxiliary engines for this purpose. The Wynfield Shipping Company of Grimbsy bought Dutch Kromhout marine diesel engines, of 70 hp and 90 hp respectively, to fit into the 140 ton "*Pioneer*" and the 200 ton "*Worrynot*". Although these ships still had a full sailing-rig, the engines fitted were by no means of modest horsepower. Wynfields were amongst the first barge company to see the way forward. They started building barges with bigger engines and smaller rigs. The "*Wessex*", of 275 tons and 30.9m in length, was fitted with a 90 hp Kromhout marine diesel engine and a much reduced sail area. Now, for the first time, it was the rig and not the engine that was the source of auxiliary power. On the continent, the 1914-18 war, out of necessity produced a flurry of engineering advancement. As far as our barge story is concerned, the most important was the two-stroke diesel engine designed for submarine work by the Sulzer engineering company. This allowed the diesel engine to advance itself once more and shortly after the war ended, the motor manufacturer Karl Benz came up with the first true fuel injection pump. This pumped pure "solid" diesel oil, rather than a compressed air and oil mix. The engines were still physically large, but were solid, reliable and hard working. The pre-World-War-II Brons single and twin engines powered literally thousands of continental motor-barges and many are reliable enough to still be in use today.

8) In 1919, this very efficient and relatively small engine was produced by Otto Deutz. It is a vertical, single-cylinder, four-stroke engine, with electric spark ignition from a magneto. It produced 6 hp at 400 rpm.

9) A Kromhout diesel motor, model 3HK4, from 1946. It is a three-cylinder engine producing 160 hp, at 325 rpm.

The 1920's were a bad time for the English coasting fleet with a recession taking hold and although the Dutch suffered a similar fate in 1929, it was the purpose-built steel motor coasters of the Netherlands that came to be the dominant force in the trade. In the face of competition from these seaworthy and fuel efficient little ships, many English coasting ships, both sail and steam were forced to adopt diesel engines earlier than might otherwise have been the case.

Sadly, the second world war was the catalyst for the next flurry of innovations. All the warring nations now needed power and more power. In aviation the Rolls Royce factory was using "exotic" alloys such as Hydaminium and sodium filled exhaust valves to aid cooling. By 1945, the Rolls Royce Merlin, supercharged aero-engine of 27 litres capacity, was producing 2000 horsepower and drinking fuel at the rate of 3.5 gallons a minute. This may seem to have little to do with barges, but after the war, the evolution of the supercharger allowed a new breed of more powerful diesel engines to appear in the larger river ships. In the smaller ships, the old Brons and the newer Kromhout three-cylinder engines reigned supreme, along with an influx of converted road units based on road-going applications. The war had seen a huge growth in the need for rugged engines for trucks and tanks and so these, mainly diesel powered units, were ideal for marinisation. BMC, MAN, Bedford, Ford, Deutz, Daimler, Mercedes, Chevrolet and General Motors, all found their way into the barges of Europe.

The diesel engine had evolved into a useful reliable tool. It was available in two- or four-stroke configuration, supercharged or normally aspirated, air or electric start. From humble beginnings at the beginning of the century, such as the single-cylinder Brons 24 hp engine, it had passed through the twin-cylinder Van Berkel 80 hp, the three-cylinder Kromhout of 160 hp, the four-cylinder Kromhout of 80 hp, the five-cylinder Ruston of 100 hp and up to what we might consider the modern configuration of the Deutz, DAF and Gardner six-cylinder engines of around 100 hp. The old engines were massive and produced their power low down in the rev range on account of their huge flywheels, around 300 revs in most cases. The modern in-line sixes, with only internal flywheels, need to run higher, at 1000 rpm or more to produce much the same power.

10) Six-cylinder Deutz, in the coaster "Zeemeeuw".

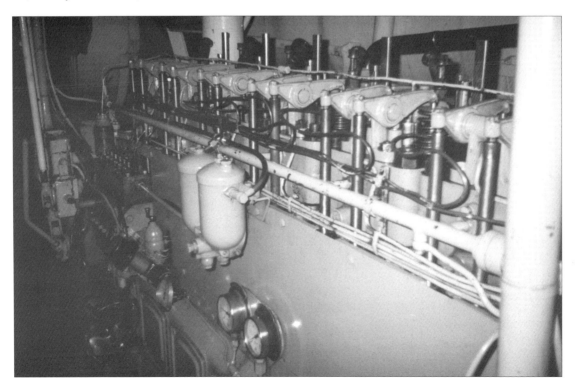

11/12) The luxemotor *"Volharding"* still has an original, fully functioning, two-cylinder Brons diesel. It is an air start engine, with an outside flywheel weighing two tons.
Note the substantial external pushrods and Brons nameplate.

Early Brons engines were built in Delfzijl, but later work was transferred to Appingedam. Engines built here are usually referred to as "Appingedammer Brons".

CHAPTER TWO

The zijschroef

In the early years of this century the internal combustion engine was making its presence felt. On land it was already powering automobiles and motor bicycles and in America it had taken to the air in the hands of the Wright brothers. In the Netherlands, as in other countries, steam tugs and ships were puffing there way around the coast, but on the inland waters the sailing-barge still reigned supreme. On the great rivers with their strong currents, steam tugs would attach themselves to as many as a dozen of these sailing freight ships and haul them, for a price, up-river. These skippers always resented paying someone else to do their work for them and if they could find ways to make their ships better they would not shrink from doing so. Steam engines were available and reliable enough to power ships, but to convert an existing sailing-ship to steam power, although it was done in isolated cases, was not practical. The steam engine took up an enormous space and then there was all the coal to carry; add the skipper and his family to the equation and you will see that there is virtually no room left for the cargo. Some very far-sighted skippers could see the possibility of utilizing a petrol or diesel powered engine to propel their ships, but the true breakthrough came, as in many cases, in a roundabout way. The ships employed in dredging for sand and gravel on the rivers in the south of the country, notably the river IJssel, had one of the hardest jobs of the binnenvaart (inland trade) fleet. The dredging was done with buckets and by hand, using only manual winches. At some point, one of these skippers placed a small petrol engine on the fore-deck of his ship and used it to power his winch. Soon everyone was employing this technique and even extending it to power the anchor winch as well. One enterprising skipper took a screw propeller and shaft from a small motorboat, hung it over the side of his ship, took a belt from the shaft to a pulley wheel on his deck-mounted engine and the zijschroef (side screw) was born. The idea was taken up and refined by engineers and side-mounted screw propellers began to spread from the southern provinces to appear all over the country.

Skippers not engaged in dredging preferred to keep their decks clear to allow them to work the sails and to load extra cargo on deck (deklast). In these cases the zijschroef installations employed an engine fitted below deck in the area of the mast. This still took up valuable cargo space however and so it was still resisted by many. Even the small engines available at the time, generating 8 or 9 hp, took up a considerable space and so it was still mainly the larger ships, over 20m or so, that fitted them.

In Germany, Rudolph Diesel had started a revolution in internal combustion technology and now the engine bearing his name was becoming available. One of the first and probably the most popular diesel engine used to power the zijschroef before the first world war was the Liggende Renes. Renes was the name of the manufacturing company in Germany and liggende refers to the horizontally mounted cylinder, or lying-down cylinder. An example of one of these single-cylinder engines can be seen at the Kromhout museum in Amsterdam. The cylinder reminds one of the barrel of a canon and the two, huge, spoked-flywheels are reminiscent of a gun carriage. This similarity to a gun is not purely coincidental, as the immense forces at work in these first engines were not so far removed from those found in a gun, with the same inherent risks. However, to a skipper and more especially his crew, embracing new labour saving technology was well worth the effort.

13) The lack of a motor often meant long hard hours for the skipper and his sons. Mother didn't escape either, she was at the helm. At least father has his pipe!

14) The klipperaak "*Disponsibel*" at anchor waiting to load cargo. She has her zijschroef lowered; the engine to drive it is located in a motor-shed on the fore-deck.

These early engines were rugged and reliable and, being diesels, once started they would keep running despite any amount of water percolating their environment. They also produced their power at low revolutions, generating good honest torque rather than the runaway mechanical motion found in many petrol engines. After the war, new Renes engines ceased to be available and spare parts also became a problem. However, new Dutch and English motors were freely available and generally these were more advanced than the early Liggende Renes. The practice of thrusting burning rags at the cylinder head had been replaced by the hot bulb gloeikopmotor (glow-head-motor), or by using a slow burning wick on the end of a plug screwed into the combustion space. Two or three-cylinder engines, with the heady output of 20 hp or greater were being fitted. Motors from the factories of the Anglo Belgian Company (ABC), Brons and Kromhout were very popular, as were the Swedish built Avance single-cylinder engine and the English Lister and Fowler twin- and single-cylinder units. Subsequently, many other engines found their way into zijschroef installations, but from beginning to end, the single-cylinder diesel engine of modest horsepower was the favourite tool for the job. The years around 1920 were the golden age for the zijschroef, although the first purpose-built luxury motor-ships had started to appear and the writing was on the wall for those who could see it. Klippers, tjalken, steilstevens and spitsen, all began to appear with the zijschroef fitted, in some cases with two or even three fitted in tandem. However, diesel fuel cost money and the wind was still free. There was not a wholesale rush by sail-skippers to cut down masts, fit wheel-houses and become motor-skippers. Some skippers did bite the bullet early on and convert their ships with a hekschroef (tail shaft) and large main engine, but this was only truly practical where the ship was large enough to justify the huge loss of space, or where power was an absolute advantage, such as on the long haul up the river Rijn from the sea and deep into Germany. The onset of the second world war was particularly bad for the pure motor-ships and those sailing-ships with full motor conversions. The Germans pressed all of these into war work and many were destroyed. The sailing-ships and those with a zijschroef were not so important to the Germans and as a result most continued to quietly continue working throughout the war. Even after the war, new zijschroef installations were being built onto existing sailing-ships.

The mechanics of the Zijschroef

Since time immemorial, ships have berthed on their left hand or port side, as the right hand side of the ship was originally encumbered by the steering oar or "steer-board" (starboard). It was natural therefore, that conventionally the zijschroef was always mounted on the starboard side of the ship. The engine was placed on, or under the deck, beside, or in line with, the mast. A belt or chain would take the driven power out onto the deck. In the case of belt drive a pulley wheel manipulated from on deck applied tension to the belt and thus acted as a clutch between engine and gearbox. When a chain was utilized, a mechanical, friction cup and cone type clutch was used. The main transmission box was mounted on the deck. In many cases the word gearbox would be a misnomer, as many installations were single-speed, single-direction transmissions. The transmission box takes the power and mechanically turns it through 90 degrees by way of a universal joint. The whole output shaft may be shifted outboard mechanically, to allow the drive-shaft to clear the side of the ship. Most installations are arranged so that the drive shaft can only operate when the shaft and propeller are in the outboard position. The exposed propeller, half in and half out of the water, is a fearsome enough beast, with the potential to snag any rope allowed anywhere near it.

15) The 22 metre klipperaak "*Friesland*" built in Zwartsluis in 1911 by the Appelo shipyard. Beneath the fore-deck is a Guldner GW 20, 19 hp, diesel engine. This is a hand start engine with a pre-heating "hot-wick", not to be confused with the hot-bulb "gloeikop" type of engine. This engine was originally fitted in 1950 to power a zijschroef installation. In 1989 the best parts of two engines were used to build one reconditioned unit. The motor also drives the anchor winch and mast winches through an intricate series of gears and clutches. The zijschroef itself has its own clutch and a forward and reverse gearbox. The unit is lowered into the water by a winch on the fore-deck.

16) Willem Jan, the co-owner and skipper of "*Friesland*", shows the "hot wick" in its holder. This is screwed directly into the combustion chamber.

Cases of zijschroeven tearing down rigging, ripping up hatch cloths, or more seriously, damaging life and limb, were by no means uncommon. The first early examples, that could turn the propeller when still on deck, must have been potentially lethal. Not for nothing did they become known as wife-killers. The drive-shaft, with a conventional screw propeller on the end, runs through a long supporting bearing that also has a brace welded to it halfway along its length. This allows the shaft to lie alongside the hull of the ship, without letting the propeller foul the ship's side. The shaft, complete with its bearing and brace, may be lifted in or out of the water by means of a tackle. In many cases this was done remotely from the cockpit, allowing the skipper to have a degree of control over the power delivery. When not in use the shaft and brace are positioned on the side-deck.

Operating a zijschroef

The zijschroef will move the ship through the water, albeit slowly, but will not provide a water flow over the rudder when getting under way. If berthed port side to, the zijschroef will initiate a turn to port almost immediately. Leaving the dockside under zijschroef power alone is not easy. A convenient wind and a good selection of long poles will work wonders in this case. When under way the ship will continually sheer to port. This is good, as it keeps the ship and the vulnerable propeller away from the shallow water at the side of the canal or river, but the downside is a distressing tendency to turn into the path of every approaching ship. There are still a half dozen or so of these installations in regular use on private ships; the skippers I have spoken to confirm this tendency, a tendency that also lead to the zijschroef being called the lamme arm (lame arm). However, one owner insists that on his ship the opposite is true and that, with the lee-board used correctly, the ship will travel in a straight line for mile after mile, better than a conventionally motorized ship with its "paddle-wheel" effect. Most ships with a zijschroef still have their lee-boards fitted. When using the zijschroef it is only possible to use the port board. This counteracts some of the thrust to port and gives the helmsman an easier time. However, if the wind is also on the port beam, a situation that on a sailing-ship would mean lowering the starboard board, then the port board and its hangings gets a tougher time, being pushed and pulled away from the hull. When passing through bridges and tunnels the utmost care is needed to protect the zijschroef and when entering a lock, judgment is everything. In most cases it is necessary to raise the shaft and propeller inboard before entering, unless the lock is empty. When the shaft is disengaged, it is down to the skipper's skill and the momentum of the ship to do the rest. There is no chance to use the engine for "one last push" and even if the propeller is left engaged to the last moment, with no astern propulsion being available in many cases, stopping can be as "interesting" as starting. At least one modern day zijschroef user has fitted an outboard motor to his rudder, with remote controls to allow a certain finesse when manoeuvreing.

The zijschroef appeared in all places and on virtually all types of ship. Tjalken, aken, klippers, steilstevens, spitsen, Kempenaars and kasten all appeared in this guise. Many different types, sizes and indeed numbers of engines were fitted and in many different ways. In some parts of the Netherlands however, it did not have such a huge impact. On areas of open water where waves and swell could be expected, such as the Oosterschelde and Westerschelde in Zeeland, the constant rolling of the ship would heave the zijschroef in and out of the water, ruining its effectiveness and possibly seriously damaging itself in the process. In open water the zijschroef was not a success.

17) This English John Fowler motor powers the zijschroef on the steilsteven "*Dankbaarheid*". Installed in 1952, it is a 16 hp unit. "*Dankbaarheid*" is one of the last binnenvaart ships built as a pure sailing-ship. Built in 1929 by the Remkes en Bodewes shipyard in Veendam, she was launched on the same day as the stock market crash in New York that precipitated a worldwide depression. Faced with a financial slump and a massive over-capacity of ships, the unfortunate owner, Dhr. Kuiper, was forced to sell her for 1500 guilders, a fraction of her original price. However, the ship survived and after spending the war years concealed in a Groningse backwater, she was fitted with a "Ridderinkhof" zijschroef in 1949 and the John Fowler motor positioned on the fore-deck. This was relocated to a space below the mast in 1952.

18) In this case the gearbox and drive unit is less complicated than on "*Friesland*". Power is simply on-off via a clutch, another lever moves the drive outboard and it is lowered by means of a cable from the wheel-house. From this remote location the skipper can also control the engine speed.

CHAPTER THREE

Pushing & Pulling

In the northern provinces, many canals were narrow and shallow, the ships were small and the zijschroef not particularly useful or popular. Praamschepen, bolschepen, boltjalken and the like, had minimal accommodation at the best of times, to lose even more space even for the advantage that a motor would give was not considered a good option. Here the smaller sailing-ships still prospered, along with the jaaglijn and scheepsjager.

The jaaglijn, or treklijn, was a line attached to the masthead of the ship, by which the ship's skipper and crew manually pulled the ship along the canal, mostly leaving the skipper's wife to steer the ship. Interestingly, the same technique was also employed in England, but here it was referred to as a "trackline". This may have been because the towpath was also a "track", but it is far more likely that the expression is simply a mispronunciation of the Dutch term.

Some smaller barges such as the snik and the pakschuit, built to carry passengers as well as cargo, were never fitted with a sail, they were designed from the outset to be towed from the canal bank. Barges built for this trade had a small solid mast built in, to provide a towing point. Sailing-barges employing a jaaglijn, had a metal collar with a hook on it that could be hauled up the mast on a halyard. The position of the towing point was all important. Too far forward and the barge would develop a sheer towards the bank from which the tow was coming. Too far aft and a sheer in the opposite direction took place. This trait could also be used to advantage however, when the nuisance caused by crosswinds could be counteracted by deliberately inducing a positive sheer, one way or the other. The jaaglijn itself was normally made from cotton, as this fibre gave a naturally springy rope, that was also strong and light.

The scheepsjager was a man with a horse who made his living from towing barges. The scheepsjager and his horse served the same function as the skipper and his son, except of course that they cost money to employ! A special breed of horse was never bred specifically for pulling barges, although a special shoe with a crossbar for extra grip was developed. Many different breeds of horse, both large and small, were employed. Most seemed to cope very well. It was the horse's temperament and stamina that was more important than anything else. The barge-horse had to be fit enough and steady enough to work a 12 or 15 hour day, often eating his meals on the move. But then again, so did the barge skipper and his crew!

In Groningen, the most famous scheepsjager was to be found alongside the Stadskanaal. This was the legendary "Job Psalm". For many years he and his faithful horse pulled ships along this canal while Job sang psalms in his deep Groningse voice. This may sound like boring monotonous work, but in fact it was fraught with dangers. A horse bolting, a ship sheering out of control, a sudden gust of wind, all could end in disaster or even death for man or beast. A Groningse newspaper from the 1st of August 1939 carried this report:

"a tragic accident occurred in which a 14 year old scheepsjager was killed. The boy was walking behind his horse, pulling a ship, when suddenly the line came loose. The fitting that the line was attached to on the ship broke free, hitting the boy in the chest, killing him instantly".

In neighbouring Friesland a motor-ship, steam-ship, or ship fitted with a zijschroef, paid twice as much in tolls as did a sailing-ship, or one being pushed or pulled by a smaller boat. This leads us to the opduwer and the opdrukker.

19) An opduwer in action pushing the ex-sailing-barge "*Anna*" on the Zuid Willemsvaart.

20) The opduwer "*Sterna*" pushes the 1042 ton sleepschip "*Suzette*"

Opduwer / Opdrukker

Two names for an essentially identical engineering solution. In the small canals of the less populated areas of the Netherlands, most skippers with small ships had to often make progress by means of poling with the vaarbomen (barge-pole) or pulling by hand or horse. They did not have the money, or perhaps more importantly the space, for any of the newfangled inboard engines, or even a zijschroef installation. When, one day, an enterprising engineer took the engine out of a model T Ford automobile and fitted it into a small canal boat, the opduwer was born. Opduwer simply means "pusher". The model T, four-cylinder, in-line, four-stroke and later the upgraded model A, were probably the first engines to succumb to a dedicated marinisation process. Certainly specialist marine gearboxes were produced specially for them. Although these boats could equally well push or pull a bigger ship, pushing was by far the most common. Pulling was reserved for the times when a string of ships needed moving. Many hundreds of opduwers were produced for use in the binnenvaart and as might be expected, many and varied uses were found for them. Around 1930, some of the northern shipyards began to produce purpose-built opduwers. These were elegant little craft, mostly between 4 and 6m long, with a scaled down hull form based on that of the steilsteven. The smaller opduwers, possibly an ex bij-boot (ship's-boot) of the Vlet or Hollandse Boot type, still tended to use petrol engines, mostly from automotive sources and intriguingly English industrial engines from Lister and Fowler, which were very competitively priced and cheaper than comparable home built engines. The larger opduwers were increasingly fitted with simple marine diesel engines from Deutz, Bolinder and Brons. The Blauwe Deutz, two-stroke diesel, in view of its relative simplicity, was very popular. In the more affluent south of the country, large 3- or 4-cylinder engines from Kromhout or Industrie provided increased horsepower. Around Rotterdam and Amsterdam, the opduwer was expected to move not just the small tjalken and aken, but also the much more massive Kempenaar and spits. For many skippers the opduwer was their first close encounter with marine engines and the more far-sighted took to full scale motorizing with enthusiasm. In 1920, 50% of the binnenvaart fleet was still under sail, by 1940 that figure had dropped to 20%. In the north it was a slower process as wages were lower, bridge and lock fees were higher for motor boats and besides, the wind still blew strongly and crucially, it cost nothing. The opduwer lost out in rough water or in strong winds in the same way as the zijschroef, but found a very useful role in the north as an icebreaker. Some were even converted with special ice-breaking bows in the manner of their huge cousins in the south of the country. When ice-breaking, the opduwer, now operating ahead of its larger partner, was remote from its parent ship and needed to be constantly crewed. When in its customary position tucked under the port quarter of its parent, the opduwer, controlled by cables and linkages from on board the larger ship, could be left to its own devices. This was a thoroughly satisfactory system and many continued in trade up until the 1960's. It soon became clear that pushing was better than pulling and many of the tugs on the great rivers were modified to this role. These were, and are, bigger ships of course and today you can see huge pusher ships with up to four dumb barges secured in pairs before them. Some of the smaller conversions are still around however and can still be found, unhurriedly and steadfastly pushing a single barge in front of them.

CHAPTER FOUR

Sailing-barge to motor-barge

Many Dutch motor-barges offered for sale for private use today are sailing-barge hulls stripped of their sailing accouterments. Most of the commercial sailing freight ships made the conversion to power successfully, some more so than others. The smaller ships were either pensioned off, to emerge once more in the present times as pleasure boats, or, if feasible, they were lengthened and deepened. When buying a motor-barge today it is important to know what the original hull was designed for and whether it has been lengthened. There are three phases in the development of the iron or steel built Dutch sailing-barge. The first is that of the tjalk and aak hull form, a design that has its roots in the middle ages. The second is that of the klipper, which appeared as an all new design around 1880. The last is that of the steilsteven and zeilkast. These two latter ships having a hull form bridging the gap between sailing-barges and the true motor-barge.

Tjalk & Aak

At the turn of the century there was a bewildering range of binnenvaart ship types. However, the vast majority of the true inland freight ships sprang from one of two very old hull forms. These were the tjalk and the aak. By the end of the nineteenth century, the tjalk was the most common of all the Dutch binnenvaart ships. The change from wooden to iron construction saw little appreciable change in the tjalk form. The use of metal rolling techniques allowed a curved bilge to be introduced, replacing the harder chine previously seen in wooden construction, but otherwise the design remained unaltered. Although the tjalk shares many features with other binnenvaart ships, they can be recognized primarily by their distinctive hull form. The curved voorsteven (stem), which also leads to them sometimes being referred to as kromstevens (bent stems) and the inward turning boeisel (the upper portion of the hull), are all indicative of the tjalk hull form. A heavy iron band, the berghout, is carried all around the hull for strength and to act as a rubbing strake. This is wide in appearance and fattens out into what are known as stuizen, at stem and stern. The bottom is flat with no keel or keelson and has a noticeably rounded bilge. If the original wooden rudder remains, it will be very large and mounted on the stern post on conventional gudgeons and pintles.

The aak is at first glance very similar to a tjalk, some variants more so than others, but an aak hull is constructed in a different way to the tjalk. The roots of this design go way back in history. As early as 800 ad, wooden aak type ships were used on the Rhine. A little later, in the sixteenth century, again on the Rhine, the aakschip known as the Keulenaar, from Keulen (Cologne), was voyaging eastwards. By the nineteenth century the predominant Rijnschip was the Dorstense aak. These ships were all long and relatively thin, lightly built and with a large spread of sail. The aak hull extends the flat central bottom plate to bow and stern, curving up to form a particularly blunt shape. In most aak forms there is no voorsteven, just the flat plate known as the heve plate. This also leads to them being called hevelaken. In a few types such as the IJsselaak and the rietaak, a voorsteven is used as well as the heve plate, these are then called stevenaken. In both types a loefbijter (a small skeg fitted to the stem) may be fitted to improve the sailing qualities.

21) The harbour in Hansweert. All trade stopped on a Saturday as the locks and bridges were closed on Sunday. So at weekends the harbours were always full. In this picture can be seen many of the sailing-barge types that successfully adapted to motorizing (tjalk, aak, klipper etc) along with the true motor-barges (spits, luxemotor, Kempenaar and beurtmotor). This harbour is, sadly, now a car park.

25

Above the berghout, at kop and kont (bow and stern), the hull plates of an aak do not in general have any inward-falling tumblehome as the tjalk does. This gives them a distinctive look that easily distinguishes them from a tjalk. Many aken were built for fishing and although built in a similar fashion to their inland cousins they were fitted with long thin lee-boards in the same way as the more well-known fishing craft, the botter.

In the case of both tjalk and aak, steering was originally carried out by means of a long heavy tiller. Many skippers seized the opportunity to convert their craft to wheel-steering with the introduction of the Engelse stuurwerk, an English steering-gear produced by John Hastie and Company, in the early part of the twentieth century. Craft so fitted can generally be identified by the way that the helmsman must steer with the wheel behind, or alongside him.

All tjalken and aken were originally fitted with a zwaard (lee-board) on each side. These were of wooden construction and had a subtle airfoil form. They were fan shaped, distinguishing them easily from the deep water craft whose zwaarden were long and thin. The sailing-rig consisted of a loose footed gaff grootzeil (mainsail) on a heavy boom, a small fok (staysail), self tacking on a horse just forward of the mast and one or more kluivers (jibs), carried on a kluiverboom (bowsprit). The use of ketch rig and top sails originally occurred only on the larger tjalken engaged in the coastal trade and the larger Rijnaken. The typical length was between 15 to 25m and the weight from 20 to 150 tons. The length to beam ratio was normally in the order of 4 or 5 to 1.

As we have seen, motorizing appeared first as the zijschroef and many ships worked with this to the end of their active life. Many others used the services of an opduwer, along with their own sailing capacity, well into the 50's. The majority of the larger ships fitted inboard engines as they became available and in most cases lengthened their ships at the same time. The round tjalk stern was not so easy to motorize as that of a klipper or zeilkast but it was generally successfully achieved. The smaller ships often needing a small skeg built in to allow the propeller to get a little extra depth and thus grip of the water. Where an engine was fitted, a wheel-house was generally built over the stern and the forward roef retained as living space. The achteronder (stern cabin), that once housed the skipper, now housed the engine. Paviljoenschepen allowed the skipper's quarters to remain, with the wheel-house now over the cockpit and engine. As late as 1988 the motortjalk "Gelria 11", built by van Goor in Zwartsluis in 1906, was still commercially active. "Gelria 11" had by then been lengthened to 38.1m by 4.75m, loading 226 tons.

Westlander

Turning away from the larger ships to the smaller end of the scale, we come to the Westlander. In the area around Maassluis, Delft and Leiden, known as the Westland, a particular type of small ship evolved. The shallow and narrow drainage canals in this area dictated, as was so often the case, the dimensions of the craft that used them. The maximum width available was 4m and even then ships with a beam of this size were less than popular, as their beam made passing and mooring difficult. The favoured beam measurement was generally around 2.5m or less. General bridge height meant that they had to achieve an air draft of no more than 1.4m. The shallowness of the canals made a fully laden draft of less than 1 metre necessary. To suit these restrictions a typical length of 15-16m evolved. They had a small roef for the skipper and hatch-boards similar to the bigger craft, but without a central supporting scheerboom (spine). They had lee-boards and a sailing-rig, but were pulled and poled as often as they were sailed.

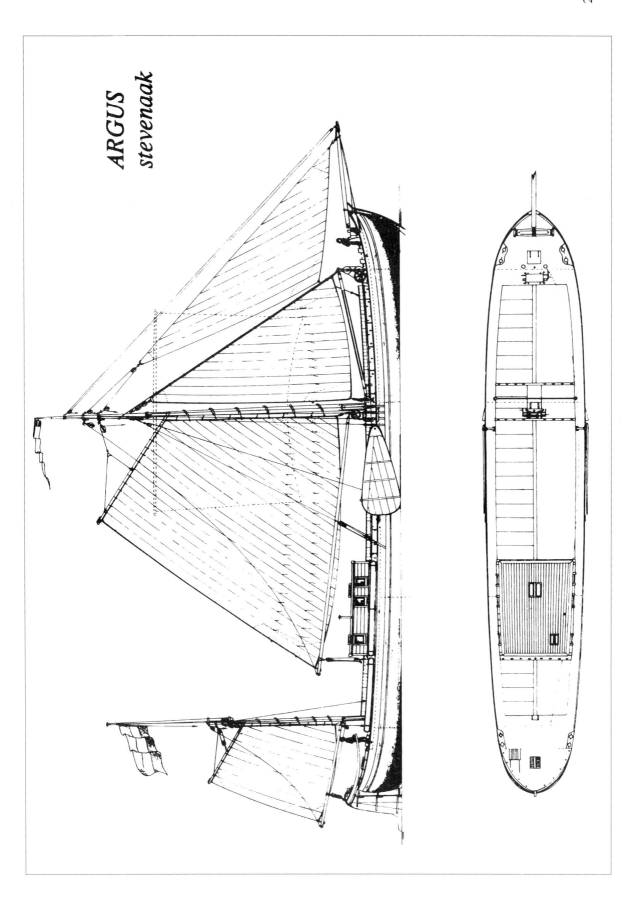

ARGUS
stevenaak

The Westlander looks a little like an aak in form, but has a very distinctive square stempost which hung on from the times when they were constructed from wood. The iron and steel Westlanders have a length to beam ratio of around 6:1 and a draft of less than a metre. To this family can also be added the vlet, Veense praam, bok, pakschuit and smaller praam types. However the Westlander eventually grew into a purpose-built motor boat and its dimensions make it broadly suitable for the canals of England, which are not generally welcoming to tjalken, aken and the like (see chapter 8).

Klipper

Probably the second most common converted sailing-barge type to be seen today is the klipper. This ship has no wooden ancestors and appeared late in the nineteenth century, constructed at first in iron and later in steel. The hull shape has its roots in the large ocean-going ships of the time and it immediately made a big impact on the binnenvaart scene. They were elegant, flamboyant, one, two, or even three-masted ships and were, without exception, all roefschepen, with an aft, open, wheel steering position. This ship is completely different to either the tjalk or the aak. With its long overhanging bow and elegant counter-stern it can not easily be confused with other types.

Kraak

The kraak came into being at about the same time as the klipper. The name kraak is an old one and goes far back in time to an 18th century, inland waters, cargo carrying, sailing-barge. The iron kraak was completely new however and owed little or nothing to its ancestor. The hull had very little sheer, was long and deep and full in the bow, with the characteristic inward turning boeisel at the kont that became known as the gebroken neus (broken nose). They had a counter-stern, less pronounced than that of the klipper, whilst still allowing wheel steering to be standard, but in this instance the wheel was mostly mounted horizontally. They varied in size as did most of the binnenvaart ships, the smallest being as little as 13m long, but the majority were 20-30m in length and displaced around 100 tons.

The kraak was a good, solid, sensible ship, carried a good load of cargo for its size, but unfortunately lacked the grace and charisma of the klipper. In many ways it was every bit as good, if not better than the river-klipper, but the sail-skippers knew what they liked and the kraak never gained much popularity outside of the southern provinces.

The chances of finding a motorkraak are very slim, but on the other hand many motorklippers exist, some still working commercially. The motorklipper "Jacoba", which I encountered in Scotland, is now working as a sand barge in Ireland. The klipper was built all over the Netherlands and was a popular ship with a certain charisma. In fact, size for size it loaded less cargo than a tjalk or aak, but its racy lines gave it greater speed. Generally speaking, the klipper in all its guises was a strongly built ship. They came in several forms, the long thin river ships, the smaller, all purpose single-masted ships and at the top end of the market, the imposing Noord-Zee klipper. These coastal ships, built to Germanisch Lloyd standards, are a better option for ambitious cruising, but the river ships with their greater length, in a narrower beam, are perhaps a better bet for canal and river work. Their efficient hull shape, up to 32m in length, originally allowed these two-masted ships to sail at least part-way up the Rhine, beyond a point where spitsen and tjalken mostly needed the services of a tugboat.

The klipper stern shape lent itself to motorizing well, much better than the round tjalk stern and many ships had inboard diesels fitted early in their lives, proportionally fewer going through the zijschroef stage. In the years between the wars many were lengthened and deepened at the same time as more powerful motors were fitted. *"Salvator"*, a sailing Klipper, was built in 1887 in Krimpen a/d IJssel, at the van den Giesen shipyard, for Jakob Katenbach from Coblenz in Germany. As a motor-barge, she was lengthened in 1930 to 44.85m by 6.96m and continued to trade commercially to the 1970's.

The Klipper hull form was recognized as being suitable for fulfilling a role as a pleasure vessel early on in its life. In his book "Barges", John Leather mentions the Klipper yacht *"Cluan"*, built for Brigadier General D. Beale-Brown. This ship was built in the Netherlands, at Nieuwendam, by G. de Vries Lentsch. Measuring 21.5m by 5m and drawing just over 1m, she was fitted from new with a 45 hp English Glenifer engine.

Because of the greater load carrying capacity of a round-hulled vessel, some skippers specified a hybrid when ordering a new ship. This was universally called a klipperaak. Most do in fact simply have an aak type stern, on what is otherwise, albeit slightly more rounded, a klipper hull. Some were built with a tjalk stern and others are simply unique.

Schoener

The klipper also developed into the schoener and schoeneraak. These were large ships, in some cases capable of world girdling, certainly some were known to trade in the Caribbean. As recently as 1997 the *"Oosterschelde"*, built in Zwartsluis in 1918, measuring 36.3m by 7.5m and displacing 260 tons, rounded Cape Horn under sail. The schoener types have a more rounded (rather than flat) bottom and no lee-boards. Very simply speaking, the twin-masted, schooner-rigged, klipper-type sea ships are traditionally (and logically) called schoeners and schooner rigged, klipperaken are called schoeneraken. Today, many a so-called motor-schoener, is in reality most likely a motor-klipper.

Steilsteven

In the early part of this century, new ship designs tended towards a steil (steep), rather than krom (bent), stem. The kromsteven was being replaced by the steilsteven. Ships built this way are all generically steilstevens. Many steamboats and all luxemotors are technically steilstevens, but one type took the name for itself. Around 1910 a new sailing freight-ship appeared. It had the back end of an aak, complete with aft tiller and open cockpit, straight sides and straight, pointed bow, similar to the newly emerging beurtmotor (see chapter 8).

The first examples were true sailing-ships, fitted with the classic wooden zwaarden and traditional grootzeil, fok and kluiver sailing-rig. Later examples tended towards cheaper, less efficient steel zwaarden and a much smaller sailing-rig, without the kluiver. The steilsteven was also built outside of the Netherlands, farther to the east in Germany and here it was sprit rigged. The German-built ships were mostly pulled by man or horse and sailed only when the wind was aft, or on the beam. All the steilstevens were lightly built, with a flat bottom and a curved bilge. The first ships tended towards a common size of 25m by 5m, but as they became established, both smaller examples for the narrow inland canals and larger for the bigger waterways were built.

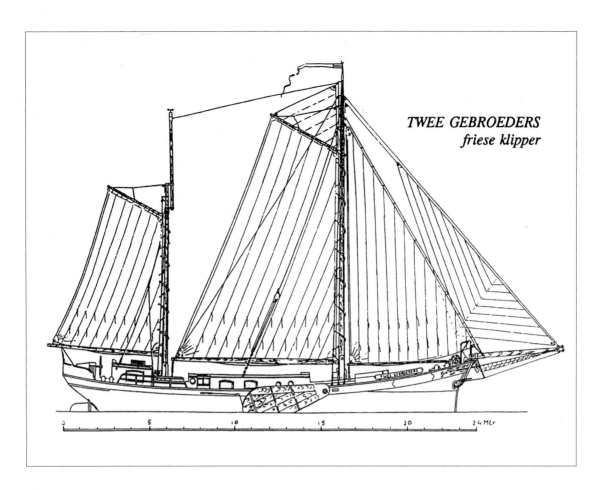

TWEE GEBROEDERS
friese klipper

23) Klipper

24) Klipperaak

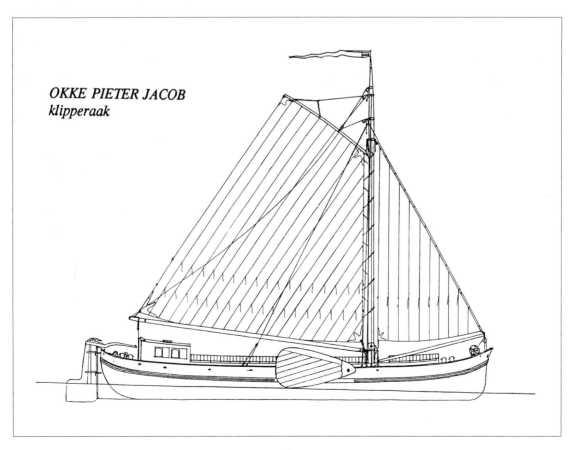

OKKE PIETER JACOB
klipperaak

The steilsteven originated in the northern province of Groningen, where they mostly carried farm produce and peat. Here they were sometimes called zeilaak or Groninger steilstevenaak. Steilstevens were eventually built all over the country and in many of the yards that were more used to building tjalken. Since many ships were built from only the most basic of drawings, individual yards tended to turn out ships that to an experienced eye were typical of that specific yard. A tjalk is very full and rounded and so, to a yard used to working this way, a straight-sided, sharp-bowed ship did not really look right. This led to some steilstevens being built to much fuller lines than others. These, mainly from the yards around the Zuiderzee, were better sea-ships although they were slower. In extreme examples a ship was built with as much as one metre difference in beam between the centre part and the ends. A "normal" steilsteven had virtually parallel sides. In the manner of a tjalk or aak they have a berghout and boeisel, but the berghout is small and carried high on the ship's side leading to an equally narrow boeisel. An original example will have a low zeilroef (a cabin built forward of the steering position),with the entrance on the starboard side in traditional Groningse fashion. The roef was small, but comfortable, with as much personal style as the skipper and wife could afford. Typically there would be a centre-piece glass fronted cabinet, with maybe a pair of matching corner units. These would have been selected by the skipper's wife before the ship was built and then "built in" to the roef by the timmerman (carpenter-joiner) as he constructed it. The interior of the roef was an expression of the skipper's wealth, pride and prestige and the attention to detail was truly painstaking. Today it is well worth seeking out and preserving these features if you are lucky enough to find them intact. The roef would normally have two side-windows, possibly with metal shutters. The sleeping cabin was under the cockpit in the achteronder and the crewman would sleep right forward in the vooronder (space under the fore-deck). By 1920 the steilsteven was beginning to adopt the motor. Older ships and many new ones still opted for an opduwer or zijschroef, but also the motorsteilsteven was built. These first motorized versions had to mount the motor in the space formally occupied by the zeilroef and a wheel-house was built on the stern of the ship where the tiller used to be. They still had a mast and sailing-rig, but it was now right forward and used mainly for loading. The only advantage in retaining the aak stern was that it gave room for a sleeping area under the wheel-house. It made more sense to use a motor-ship stern as well as the established straight motor-ship bow, fit a wheel-house over the engine-room and a salonroef, as seen on the new luxemotor types, aft of the wheel-house. Now the steilsteven was effectively just one more beurtmotor and no longer a sailing-ship. By 1930 no more steilstevens were built. Paradoxically, one of the last, if not <u>the</u> last steilsteven built, was a true sailing-ship with no motor at all. The *"Dankbaarheid"*, built in 1929 with small sailing-rig and basic steel zwaarden, somehow survived the "crisis" years of 1929-31 and after being hidden in an isolated Groningse canal during the war to escape requisition by the Germans, *"Dankbaarheid"* was fitted with her first engine. This is a John Fowler twin-cylinder diesel of 20 hp driving a single speed zijschroef.

A motorized steilsteven is a perfectly capable little ship, but it must be remembered that they are not so strongly built as a luxemotor and the older ships, with a true aak stern, were designed to handle best under sail and with zwaarden to help them manoeuvre.

25) A diversity of ships with a common trade in IJmuiden.
From left to right: Hagenaar, klipper, beurtmotor, tjalk, Katwijker.

26) The motorijsselaak *"Jenny"*, note how the sides of the hold have been raised to allow a greater tonnage to be loaded.

Zeilkasten

In the west of the Netherlands, on the great rivers and in the harbours, there was a constant trade carried on by sleepschepen. These were basically ships that were designed to be pulled or pushed, rather than travel under their own power (see chapter 6). Those sleepschepen that traded on the rivers and canals of France and Belgium only developed a very limited sailing capability (see "spits", chapter 7). In the north of the Netherlands the landscape was predominantly flat, with large areas of semi-open water. Here it made sense to make use of the available wind, after all the wind was still free and a horse was no good in the middle of a lake! Large fleets of both kasten and zeilkasten developed here (similar to sleepschepen. See chapter 6). The "Rederij Zwaak" (the "Zwaak" shipping company) in Friesland had an impressive fleet of Friese sleepkasten known as the "Zwakies". The zeilkast first appeared, built of iron, around 1880 and had a rectangular sleepschip hull, but with a bow and stern resembling that of the klipper, although the counter was not so pronounced. The early ships actually looked very good with their full sailing gear, wooden zwaarden and flowing lines.

A typical example is the" *"Zwerver"*, a Friese Maatkast (a kast normally built to specific Friese measurements), built in 1912, by the "Boot" shipyard in Gouwsluis, for Dhr. Visser. *"Zwerver"* measured 31.5m by 6.26m, lee-boards excluded. Dhr. Visser did not intend to trade in Friesland, so the wider beam that he specified, too wide for many of the Friese locks, was not a problem. He skippered this ship under sail until 1938, when an 150 hp Industrie engine was fitted. 25 years later, in 1963, *"Zwerver"* had grown to 49m in length and now loaded 499 tons compared to her original 250 tons. A 380 hp Deutz took the place of the Industrie and *"Zwerver"* began a new career as a passenger ship on the Rhine.

Zeilkasten were large roefschepen with a horizontal and later vertically mounted wheel. Because of the length of the hull, the mast had to be fitted to a central mastdek, thus splitting the cargo hold into two sections. As in most other cases, as the years progressed and modern mechanical methods of loading became available, it was necessary to move the mast, now used only as a crane, to the fore-deck.

The standard size for a zeilkast was 31m by 5.5m. This was the maximum size that would still allow them to use the "zeesluizen" of the Zuiderzee and Waddenzee ports. Ships built to these specific dimensions were called Friese maatkasten (Friese measurement kasten). The Friese maatkast is not specifically a ship type. It is merely a standard of measurement, as was the case of the spitsmaat in Belgium.

In Friesland the canals were divided into four categories, each with its own maximum allowable size limit. The dimensions of the zeesluis at Stavoren were 32.5m by 7.6m, thus dictating the upper limit for class 1.

class 1)   31.5m by 5.4m.

class 2)   21.5m by 3.8m.

class 3)   18.2m by 3.3m.

class 4)   14.9m by 2.8m.

27) The heavily laden zeilkast *"Hoop en Vertrouwen"* with severely reduced sail entering Lemmer on the Zuiderzee (later to become the IJsselmeer).

28) Lemmer again and this time it is the tjalk *"Aaltje"* that is entering in strong winds.
On the IJsselmeer, strong winds and shallow water soon build into nasty sailing conditions.

"I have sailed all over the world, but the worst weather is on the IJsselmeer".
Skipper Ynze Scheffer, from Urk.

The zeilkast did not survive the crisis years and no more were built after 1930. Many existing ships were motorized very successfully. Their large size and counter-stern made the fitting of an engine much easier than in the case of the rounded stern ships. Those that were converted tended to build a wheel-house over the cockpit and keep the forward zeilroef. After the war many were lengthened and deepened and may still be seen in trade today. The *"Maria Debora"* was built in 1892 with zwaarden and full sailing-rig. By 1980 she had been lengthened to 75m and was now loading 1000 tons compared to her original 300 tons.

Very few of the smaller zeilkasten are to be found today, but if one is available, especially the later Groningse built ones, they are strongly built and should make good motor-barges.

Motorized sailing-barges in practice

All the motor-barges on the water today as pleasure vessels, whether converted sailing-ships or purpose-built motor-barges, are fulfilling a role substantially different from that envisaged by the designer. Commercial barges had one prime motive, to move as much cargo as possible, as efficiently as possible. Comfort, although still important to the skipper, was not the number one priority. Today, it is probably true to say that a non-commercially operated barge puts home comforts at the top of the agenda. I have already mentioned the possible drawbacks of using a barge in such a way and in different geographical locations, that are greatly at odds with its original purpose. But, it is also true, that even using the barge in the manner in which it was intended to be utilised, in its original location, can still cause problems. Simply because in so many cases the operating environment has changed dramatically. A big, black, tar-sided barge, with lumps of wood as fenders, shoving its way into a crowded lock, or rafting up with four or five other barges alongside a wharf, is a different proposition to the same vessel fifty years later, being navigated in an environment full of small plastic cruisers. In a later chapter I will discuss my experiences of operating a luxemotor, but here I will restrict myself to the motorized sailing-barge. With the exception of the klipper and other types with a counter-stern, the vast majority of sailing-barge conversions are of the round-bowed, round-sterned, tjalk-type hull form. They may simply be a broadly unchanged sailing-barge with a motor, or they may have lost all their rig and gained substantial superstructure. In the first case, stability and sea-keeping will remain more or less as it always was, bearing in mind the type of craft concerned and its area of operations. My own 17.5 metre tjalk fits this category and used more or less as the builders intended, it is a good compromise between commercial and pleasure use. In disturbed waters, even if under motor, a modest amount of sail aloft goes a long way to help in reducing rolling. When navigating purely under motor, in this case a DAF 475 of 100 hp, the ship behaves very well with no bad vices. Since the ship is sailing light all of the time, i.e. no cargo is carried, the body of the ship is not deeply immersed and the propeller is not as deep in the water as it ideally could be (the plus point here is that in case of fouling the propeller, I can reach it from our dinghy and cut away bags, rope, nets, etc). If the sea is particularly lumpy there are times when the prop lifts clear of the water, but not for long enough to cause racing. Cavitation will occur at these times however. In still water cavitation is not a worry. The tjalk-type rudder is a very large item, meant to exert maximum pressure on the water when sailing. This is a benefit when motoring, as the large immersed area allows the prop wash to be usefully controlled and directed. This, coupled with correct use of the lee-boards makes for a very manoeuvreable little ship, even without a bow-thruster.

With the helm hard over and a burst of power applied, the ship will want to turn around a point about a third of the way forward of the propeller, with the appropriate lee-board lowered (that is the one on the *outside* of the turn, port when turning to starboard and starboard for port), the ship can be encouraged to turn virtually on its own axis. Depending on the direction of rotation of the propeller this will be easier one way than the other. A left handed propeller, that is one that turns anti-clockwise when viewed from astern, will initiate a tighter turn to starboard than port; the so-called paddle-wheel effect. Going astern is also relatively easy. Initially the prop-wash will cause the stern to turn in the same direction as the propeller, but here once again the huge surface area of the rudder will allow the ship to be straightened up quickly. With both lee-boards partially lowered the ship can be made to handle almost as well astern as in forward propulsion. Wind is of course the enemy, as all unladen barges tend to behave a little like a leaf on a pond. Lee-boards will go a long way to controlling this trait and if the boards are still there on your chosen project, think more than twice before removing them. Many sailing-barges that converted to full motor propulsion retained their lee-boards until the introduction of bow-thrusters.

29) The motorklipper *"Johanna"* carried sand and gravel and was fitted with a 65 hp Kromhout engine in 1937. She retains the original "zeilroef".

The second category of converted sailing-barge to be considered is one that has lost all of its sailing potential. The mast and gear has gone, allowing the metacentric height (see below), which is all important in stability and rolling issues, to increase beyond original design parameters. This is not really a problem in sheltered waters, but should be taken into consideration when contemplating open-water passages. In any case, for pleasure use, a superstructure of some kind will possibly have been added above the height of the original hatch-boards, causing a reduction in metacentric height. If a small mast still allows a steadying sail to be carried, all well and good, however, a lightly laden ex-sailing-barge hull, with no lee-boards, is less than ideal in confined space manoeuvreing situations. In this case a bow-thruster is a sensible addition.

Ballast, Metacentric height & Rolling

This is not meant to be a thesis on marine engineering, but the enjoyment and safe navigation of an ex-trading barge can be severely impaired by inappropriate conversions. This may lead to an uncomfortable motion in disturbed water. This type of water can be found on rivers and larger canals and is not just reserved for open waters.

In simple terms, metacentric height is the perpendicular distance between the centre of gravity and a notional point known as the metacentre, about which the centre of buoyancy of a ship moves at small angles of inclination (10-15°). In an upright, stable vessel, the centrer of gravity will be above the centre of buoyancy and the metacentre will lie above this in the same vertical plane. This gives a positive metacentric height.

It can be seen that this metacentric distance will increase and decrease as the centre of gravity and, to a lesser degree the centre of buoyancy, changes. This happens when a ship is in loaded or unloaded condition, or most importantly when top-weight such as masts and rigging are removed. Although they only contribute perhaps 5-7 % of the overall weight of the ship, because of their distance from the centre of gravity, their "leverage" effect is greater.

If a vessel has a large metacentric height any alteration of the water-level on either side of the ship will cause the ship to move as it tries to remain perpendicular to the surface of the water. As it says in the Admiralty Manual of Seamanship, *"this motion will be continuous, non-uniform and uncomfortable"*. A large metacentric height will make for high initial stability, a "stiff vessel", which at the same time can become unsteady when in motion. Large metacentric heights are generally seen on still-water craft like river-barges or paddle-steamers. A sailing-barge is designed with a relatively large metacentric height to give high initial stability. This means that with the sails raised and a beam wind the ship will not heel excessively.

If, on the other hand, the metacentric height is low, the righting forces acting upon the vessel are also small. At rest the ship may be "tender", that is to say that she will move easily to weights moved around the deck, but in a sea-way any rolling that does occur tends to be uniform and not too uncomfortable.

N.B. It is a common fallacy that adding ballast will stop a ship from rolling. It will achieve greater initial stability, but at the same time render it more "stiff" and thus increase her unsteadiness in disturbed water. It was well-known amongst the open-water sailing-barge skippers, that if a cargo such as gravel was carried, it must be kept low and spread out in the bilge to maintain stability. These old skippers also knew, that if too much cargo was carried too low down, the boat would become stiff and any subsequent rolling could become so intense as to shake the mast out.

Why does rolling occur anyway? Rolling in a ship is analogous to a garden swing being pushed. The time taken for the swing to complete its movement from one extreme to the other and back again is its "period". The time taken for a ship to move from one extreme of inclination to the other and back again is also its "period" or "periodic time". When force is applied to the swing in a regular way, i.e. the applied force matches the period of the swing, the extent of motion is increased. Energy is added to the motion. The same applies to barges. When an outside force, a wave train, applies energy in a regular way and this matches the period of the barge it will increase the motion. Changing heading will often stop the rolling, as the applied force no longer matches the ship's period.

There are many other factors to take into account such as inertia, skin friction, beam and hull shape, but the inescapable fact is that barges roll. They have been rolling their way around almost every corner of the world for thousands of years and no doubt will continue to do so. However, steps can be taken to minimize this discomfort and armed with just a little knowledge, modifications can be undertaken in such a way as to avoid any increase in discomfort.

30) The Hagenaar *"Johanna"* was built in 1898 in Waspik. She was converted to a motor-barge in 1945.

CHAPTER FIVE

Construction & conversion

Virtually every type of sailing-barge ever built has been successfully motorized at some time or another. Although now some types are more common than others, it is worth looking at the main types, along with their positive and negative features, to allow a sense of perspective when contemplating purchasing one for private use. It is said that a little knowledge is a dangerous thing, but in this case a little knowledge may save you money and even keep you out of danger.

All Dutch barges were built sufficiently robustly to travel safely on the inland waterways. It was their purpose. Some were built a little stronger to safely trade on the exposed waters of the Zuiderzee and the Ooster- and Wester-Schelde. Others were able to venture north into the Baltic, west over the North Sea to England and south to the Mediterranean. If the intended use of a converted sailing-ship is only on sheltered waterways, then given the usual care taken when buying a boat, whichever of the many little ships available takes your fancy will probably serve you well. If you want to cross the channel and travel Europe a little more adventurously, a bit more care is called for. This is not intended as a "barge buyers guide"; the Dutch Barge Association produce an excellent little book with that title already (see bibliography). In any case, a competent surveyor is your best friend at a time like this. What I can do is lay out the types you may encounter and tell you what their makers intended them to withstand, albeit in many cases 100 years ago!

If you wish to know more about sailing-barges, I refer you to my earlier work, "The Dutch Barge Book" (see bibliography).

At the lighter-build end of the market are the physically small tjalken and aken, the bol types and the praam types. The smaller ships, 14-18m in length, are paradoxically often better equipped to withstand abuse than their bigger brothers. A small ship is less likely to flex and has a shorter length to dry out on. What they will not like is big seas and since by and large very few barge skippers like big seas either, this is not a problem. It is when we get to the 18-24 metre range that great care is advised. There are many praam type barges that were never intended to cross open water. The turf praam was purposely built lightly, to penetrate the peat bogs of the north and still return with a worthwhile tonnage of cargo. These may be relatively large ships, but they are built from wide plates on widely spaced frames. Others were intended to trade on the Zuiderzee and their correspondingly stouter build, more plates, more frames and a strong sheer will reflect this. The bol type of ship has the same features as the praam regarding strength, but it is a plus point that many bollen where built in Groningen. Any ship built in Groningen tended to be more robustly built than a similar ship built elsewhere. From Friesland comes the skutsje. There are a great many of these for sale as both sailing and motor-barges. They were built lightly, especially the more recent 1920's steel ships and in the "worse" cases have virtually no sheer and very low freeboard. Those that travelled on the Zuiderzee are immediately obvious by the taller bow and noticeable sheer. The larger Friese built ships are strong and within their intended sphere of operation, seaworthy. The Groninger tjalk too is a very desirable base for a conversion as far as strength goes. The largest aak built was the Hasselteraak at around 22m. These are also strong, but few now remain. Of the other aak variants, those with a structural stem, the IJsselaak and rietaak for example offer a more robust construction.

There are only three variants of tjalk that were truly built as sea ships. These are, when built to a specified standard, the Groninger tjalk, the zeetjalk and the koftjalk. All these ships strongly exhibit all the following features:

1) A good solid berghout, widening out at bow and stern.
2) Deep bulwarks and wide side decks.
3) A high stem and stern.
4) Massively solid appearance.

They were built with extra frames and stringers to the highly demanding Germanisch Lloyds specification for sea ships. Barges at sea have the same problems as bulk carriers or oil tankers. They are basically a single decked vessel, a great steel box. When seas are encountered with a long period, i.e. the distance between succeeding wave troughs, the ship is subjected to hogging and sagging forces. When the middle is supported on a wave crest, the two ends are left unsupported: hogging. When the two ends are supported and the centre left unsupported, sagging takes place. A little bending is no bad thing as a ship that refuses to give, or work, will soon break up, but extreme bending will also cause the ship to fail. These are forces not normally encountered by barges. Steel ocean-going bulk carriers adopted the Isherwood system, using a great number of longitudinal stringers running fore and aft to prevent hogging and sagging. The, by comparison, smaller iron and steel barges did likewise and trade continued safely. These ships were the workhorses of the Netherlands coaster trade at the turn of the century.

If you are lucky enough to acquire one of these and the original zeilroef is still fitted, it will have an entrance on both port and starboard and if you are really lucky a compass behind a glass window in the aft facing end. If you are told that any particular ship is a zeetjalk, or koftjalk, or Oostzeetjalk, treat this information with caution. For obvious reasons they are particularly desirable ships and many unworthy ships gain this title. Bear in mind that a lightly built skutsje of 24m in length, may actually be longer than a zeetjalk. Length is not everything as they say!

There is one test that will prove that a ship is a sea ship. That is to look at the original log book or "Meetbrief". This will call a spade a spade, or in this case a zeetjalk. But what if the meetbrief appears to have been altered or is unavailable? Every ship in trade before the second world war was registered with a unique number assigned to it (see chapter 10). They all, without exception, carried this number somewhere on them. Of course it may have vanished in the conversion, but owners tend to be proud of the number and if it is still on the Dutch register, even as a pleasure vessel, it must display this original number. Normally this is found on the centre line towards the stern of the ship, on the side or back of the roef, or on the deck of the paviljoen. In the case of my own tjalk, *"Jan Willem"*, this number is 238 B AMST 1927. This means that *"Jan Willem"* was measured and registered (but not built) in 1927, in Amsterdam. It was the 238th ship registered that year and the all important B stands for Binnenvaart (inside trade). Those ships and only those ships registered for sea going trade, would, instead of the B have a Z. It is this Z for Zeevaart that tells the tale. No Z; no authorized sea trade. Having said this, not every ship that ventured on to the sea had the necessary zeebrief authorization. A skipper took trade where he found it and would not turn down a cargo lightly.

Iron & Steel

Metal shipbuilding came to the binnenvaart in the first half of the 19th century. It did not generally become common in the construction of barges (except for the dumb-barges) until the later years however. Speaking very loosely, iron was beginning to find favour with both the shipyards and the skippers around 1870 and steel appeared only 10 years later. However iron remained the primary building medium until the start of the next century and only disappeared from the scene after the first world war. Around the turn of the century many wooden ships were successfully over-plated with iron. These were called "Compositieschepen". Across the North Sea in England many sailing-barges were constructed in a composite form from new, i.e. wooden decks and planking over steel framing.

Iron, and by this I mean a type of wrought iron called "puddelijzer" in the Netherlands, was embraced gladly by the shipbuilders and most of the existing ship types then made from wood took up a new life as iron ships. Wrought iron has strengths and weaknesses as does steel. In reality they are both alloys, with steel having more carbon and other useful elements. It is often said that iron will shatter in an impact, whereas steel will bend. Most of us will have seen how easy it is to break an iron casting for example. In fact in the early days of iron shipbuilding and also in the construction of bridges, a type of iron known in the Netherlands as "gietijzer" was used. This was basically cast-iron and there were several instances of catastrophic failure. A cast-iron bridge, across the river Seine in Paris, broke in half in 1850. One of the enemies of cast-iron is frost and freezing temperatures, at these times the material becomes very brittle indeed. This is cast-iron however and by 1890 or so most shipyards were using wrought iron or puddelijzer. Although not as flexible and resilient as true steel, wrought iron is nevertheless more malleable and less prone to fracture when frozen.

You only have to look at the signs of numerous impact to be found on these 100 year old vessels to appreciate that they will not crack open on hard contact with a dockside. In any event the vast numbers of iron ships still trading, let alone in use as pleasure ships, tells us a lot about their longevity. Another myth is that iron will not rust. Unfortunately this is not true, but it does decay at a much slower rate than steel. Steel became available as smelting techniques improved. This higher quality metal had a greater tensile strength than iron, although it was more expensive. The old skippers did their sums and found that although quantity for quantity, steel was more expensive than iron, a smaller amount of steel than iron was needed to build the same size of ship.

So, an iron ship could load say 80 tons, but a similar size steel ship could load 100 tons. Extra cargo equalled extra profit and steel took over from iron. But, as we saw earlier, steel rusts more quickly than iron and since the steel plates used were thinner, a steel ship would need re-plating sooner than its iron counterpart. Whatever the pros and cons, steel was an easier metal to work than iron, weighed less to handle and could be welded. The shipyards preferred it and by 1918 iron barges were no longer built.

Records from a barge building shipyard in Groningen show that they built :

Iron ships from	1865 to 1910 with the peak building year being	1896
Combined Iron and steel ships 1878 to 1914	.. .. ..	1898
Steel ships	1878 to 1920	1902

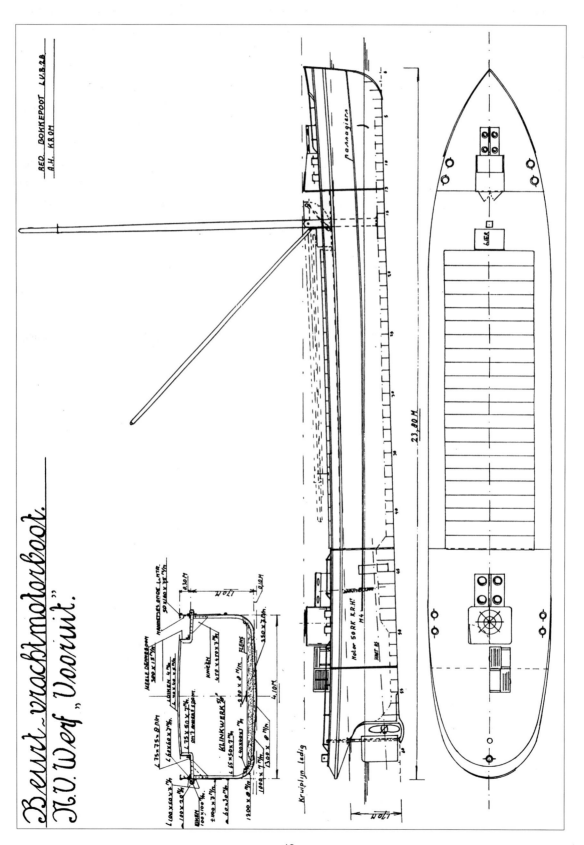

Beurt~vrachtmotorboot.
N.V. Werf „Vooruit".

31)
Beurtmotorschip, by
A. H. Krom.

42

Prior to the introduction of the pure motor-ship, barges were built to specifications laid down by the owners, skippers or shipyards. The shipyards would give the minimum scantling sizes, and depending on the finances of the owner and the advice of the skipper, based on the proposed area of use, a plan was drawn up. Typically a small inland craft like a tjalk would have plating thickness between 5 and 6 mm, a bigger barge that would be expected to occasionally cross open water might have plates 6 to 7 mm thick and a sea going ship, built to the special Germanisch Lloyd or Veritas specification would be 7 to 8 mm or thicker. When the Luxemotor appeared around 1920, the sea going versions had plates of 8 to 10 mm, their inland cousins 6 to 8 mm and the smaller beurtschepen 6 or 7 mm plates.

The zeetjalk "Wilhelmina" provides a good example of owner involvement with building. The original paperwork is now in the Prinz Hendrik Maritiem museum in Rotterdam. The commissioning owner, Dhr. Velenga came from Zoutkamp in the northern province of Groningen. Groningen is were most zeetjalken were built, however Dhr. Velenga chose instead "de zijl" ship-building and repair wharf in Leiderdorp on the Oude Rijn, situated just outside the town of Leiderdorp, in the province of Zuid-Holland. Zuid-Holland had a good reputation as far as shipbuilding went, but the typical Zuidhollandse ship was the paviljoentjalk, designed for the delta areas farther south. In any event Dhr. Velenga obviously had faith in the yard and as it was run under the umbrella of the gebroeders "Boot", who owned many successful shipyards, he had ample cause to believe in the yard's capabilities. He knew exactly what he wanted and working in conjunction with the shipyard a detailed plan and building contract was drawn up. The contract was signed in September 1902 and the finished ship was delivered less than 5 months later, in January 1903, for a cost of 7300 guilders. The ship was to be a zeetjalk, with a length of 25m and a beam of 5.6m. It was to be built of steel with iron frames and stringers. The specifications for the plating show that the bottom and bilge area was to be of 8 mm plate, the sides up to the berghout 7 mm thick and the plating beneath the berghout a solid 10 mm thick.

The side decks were to be of 5 mm plate, the deck knees to be 25 cm by 25 cm and 7 mm thick, whilst the den (the hold coaming), would be 40 cm high and 6 mm thick. All other measurements and scantling dimensions are given, right down to two gangplanks and a flagstaff.

Repairing & Replacing

After 50 to 100 years of use, most barges will need repairing. Metalwork above the waterline can be tackled in two ways:
1) a doubler can be used; this is a patch of new metal welded over the old.
2) the damaged metal can be cut away and replaced with a new section. If looks are important, then this is the only option.

 To do this, the old metal must be cut away without damaging the internal frames. If the area is an accommodation area, or if the ship has already been converted, then fire in the internal cladding is a very real risk. The favoured way is to cut part-way with a grinder or torch and finish the job with an industrial jigsaw. An exactly measured plate can then be fitted by welding to the abutting plates and by plug-welding through to the frames.

Below the waterline a doubler is probably the best option. This plate must overlap the worn or damaged area sufficiently to allow a safe weld and as before it must be plug-welded at intervals to prevent unsupported areas. Another problem here is that of water getting behind the doubler plate.

The outside welded joint may be secure, but since there is possibly damaged plating beneath it, rainwater or condensation may find ingress from within the ship. This means that the original plating must be made watertight before the new strengthening doubler is added. Because of these problems, doubling is not officially allowed on commercial craft in the Netherlands.

Riveting

Riveting was, and in its classic form still is, an intensive and highly skilled job. A good shipyard employed a large, full-time gang of riveters, for whom there was no shortage of work. There are two basic forms of rivet joint: lap-joints, where the plates overlap each other and but-joints, where the two plates are butted together and a third smaller backing plate is riveted to them both. Both appear in typical barge construction. A rivet joint is made by the contracting action of the hot rivet and the frictional forces of flat plates. A good joint will not leak, but will allow a small amount of movement as the ship "works". The larger zeetjalken sometimes needed a small amount of caulking between the joints, as the forces exerted by the sea, as opposed to lakes and canals, were proportionally greater. The best rivet joint is made by drilling the two plates together, this ensures a good fit for the rivet and does not damage the surrounding metal. In some restricted areas this was not possible and so cold punching, followed by reaming, was employed. This could cause work hardening and localized cracking at a later time and so the process was only to be found in a very few, non critical, areas of the ship. After the plates were drilled, they were bolted temporarily into position and the riveting could start. A rivet-boy would tend the fire and ensure that a ready supply of red-hot rivets was available. Rivets were initially of soft iron, with a tensile strength of around 23 tons per square inch. Later steel rivets increased this strength to 25 tons per square inch. Different application demanded different types of rivet such as cone, countersunk, roundhead, flathead and shovelhead. Each job required a specialist rivet-hammer and dolly to fit the size of rivet in use. The rivet was picked up by tongs and deftly fitted into place; a metal dolly was held against the head of the rivet, and the tail, on the outside of the two plates, was quickly beaten into shape by two men hitting alternate strokes. Riveting was a very labour intensive process. In areas such as the stem and stern-posts, where there was no room to swing a hammer, cold riveting was employed, using a pneumatic or hydraulic riveting machine. This produced an initially quick hammering action, that slowly decreased as the rivet was formed. These machines could deliver 700 blows a minute at a pressure of 30 tons. On some ships, the rivets below the waterline were countersunk to provide greater streamlining, but this was by no means standard practice and as was so often the case, available finance dictated standards of refinement.

The original plates in all the barges that we are interested in are all held in place with rivets. Otherwise sound plating can be let down by rotten rivets (nail sickness as the Dutch call it). A rivet may have a sound head and underneath a rotten shank, or conversely a sound rivet may have its head pulled off by the jacking action of rust between overlapping plates. Where a head has failed is pretty obvious, but it takes a knowledgeable surveyor to spot other problems. It is not always a quick fix to simply weld a new head onto a broken rivet, the primary cause of failure must first be addressed. If considering a re-riveting job it is useful to remember that the length of the rivet should be the thickness of the plate(s), plus 150% for ordinary rivets and plus 75% for countersunk.

It is important that the engineers and welders employed in any repair fully understand the nature of the task. On a ship that may well be over 100 years old you may find the original wrought iron structure, with later, gas welded, iron or steel plating repairs or modifications. You will almost certainly find relatively modern mild steel doublers in one area or another which have been electrically welded in place. These grades of metal and welding rods all have a different galvanic potential and consequently corrosion is guaranteed. Add to this perhaps a stainless steel propeller shaft and a manganese bronze propeller and the options for disaster grow considerably. Thankfully, galvanized steel, galvanized wrought iron, mild steel and wrought iron are all fairly close in terms of nobility on the galvanic scale. The careful use of the right welding rods for the chemical composition concerned, coupled with judicious use of anodes (magnesium for fresh water and zinc for salt water), can keep all this under control. Whilst there are undoubtedly excellent boat repair yards in England, generally speaking the Dutch, Belgian and French yards know these ships inside out.

CHAPTER SIX

The Rhine, Danube & Raderschepen

Nearly all of the ship-types in this book were to be found, at some time or another, plying their trade on the great rivers of north-west Europe. Of all the rivers, the one that figures time and time again in their story is the river Rhine. In recent years the Danube has also become more important. The strange thing is, that if you study a map of the Netherlands or Belgium, you will not find the spot where the Rhine meets the sea. Neither will many atlases show that the Rhine and Danube are now connected. If you turn your mind back to your days in geography class, you may remember something about the Lek, the Waal and the Maas. Possibly even something about the continental divide. Forgive me then if I refresh your memory and explain the extent, and because of this the importance, of the great rivers Rhine and Danube. (A map, or navigational chart if you have one, might be handy at this point).

The headwaters of the rivers and streams that supply the Rhine come from the watershed area of the continental divide in Bavaria. From this region the waters can either run west towards their eventual merging with the North Sea, or they can flow south-east towards the Black sea. To the west the Rhine is the major watercourse and to the east, the river Danube. Both these rivers have always been important to trade and as long ago as 793 AD, the Emperor Charlemagne set his men to digging a canal to join the rivers Altmuhl and Schwabische Rezat, to create an unbroken waterway of some 2000 miles linking the Black Sea to the North Sea, east with west. In the event he failed, having been defeated by the terrain itself and the need to be off elsewhere, protecting and enlarging his empire. It was 1845 before the next attempt occurred. King Ludwig 1 of Bavaria had the first successful Danube-Main canal built, but with lock dimensions of less than 5m width it could not take the larger river ships then operating on the two great rivers. This unfortunate fact, added to very poor management, ensured that it was never a success. In 1921 a new company was formed. The firm of Rhein- Main- Donau AG, slowly ate away at the problems involved and after 70 years of deliberating, planning and negotiating, the Danube-Rhein canal became a reality. This 55 metre-wide canal runs for 106 miles and rises through 246m by way of massive flights of ship-locks. A "Eurobarge" carrying up to 3000 tons can now travel from Rotterdam, through Germany, Austria, Hungary, Romania, the former Yugoslavia and Bulgaria, before emerging into the Black sea. A journey literally across a continent. Still, however tempting it might be to continue our story eastwards, it is to the west we must look and get back to the Rhine.

Interested readers can learn more about this canal by reading the book written by Bill and Laurel Cooper entitled "Back door to Byzantium", A&C Black, ISBN 0-7136-4637-3. Bill and Laurel with their Luxemotor "Hozanna" successfully attempted the passage in 1996/97.

The first thing to establish is the proper spelling of the name, as the river winds its way to the sea it changes its spelling and indeed its name several times. For navigable purposes the Rhein (German spelling), starts at Rhein Felden in Switzerland. River traffic has a short run to Basel, where barges must take the Canal du Rhone au Rhin (French spelling). This canal leads to Kembs-niffer, where a change of canal to the Grand canal D'Alsace parallels the river, to rejoin what is now the Rhein at Breisach. From here it is all "down hill" as the river picks up water from the Alps and speeds westwards for almost 500 miles (830K). The next large towns are Strasbourg and then Manheim, where the river Neckar flows in to join the Rhein. A little farther on is Mainz, where the river Main adds its weight to the flow and then Koblenz, where the waters are swelled once more by the Mosel and Lahn.

32) "Hold this tight" said the father of Paulus van Wekhoven and that is just what he did !

Now the river speeds towards Bonn and Köln. The last river to merge with the Rhein in Germany is the Ruhr, which adds its volume at Duisburg. The final town in Germany supplied by the Rhein is the border town of Emmerich. A few miles west of here the river enters the Netherlands and becomes the Rijn (Dutch spelling). Just before it leaves Germany it splits in two.

The south flowing section becomes the Waal and the remainder heads for Arnhem, where it splits again to become the north flowing Gelderse IJssel, merging with the IJsselmeer at Kampen. The remaining water flows on westward through Arnhem and from this point it is known as the Nederrijn, flowing almost parallel to its sibling the Waal. The Nederrijn flows through the low-lying green countryside of Gelderland to Wijk bij Duurstede, where it suddenly and arbitrarily changes its name to the Lek and runs on to Rotterdam. Meanwhile the Waal, making its own way west, comes to Dordrecht and divides again to form the Oude Maas, which joins the Lek at Rotterdam, whilst the Waal itself heads a little more south to join the Maas in the Hollandse Diep.

From its headwaters close to the Alps, where currents run at 4-8 kts and much faster when in flood, to the wide, shallow, slow flowing, river in the Dutch Delta region, the Rhine is a natural if somewhat hazardous highway. Barges from Germany, Belgium, the Netherlands, Switzerland and Luxembourg all have easy access to it. Ships have navigated it since Roman times and no doubt even earlier than that. It was 1816 however, before the first powered craft, a steamboat, reached Germany from Rotterdam. It was almost 100 years later, in 1904, before the first steam tug reached Bonn with a train of "sleepschepen" in tow and from that time onwards, a barge that could not cope somehow with the river Rhine was severely disadvantaged. From England, the Thames barges carried white clay to the potteries at Bonn and returned with coal or Appolinaris water. Sand and gravel are still dredged and carried both up and down river, huge double-decker car carriers, long, chunky, scrap-metal lighters and as always tons and tons of coal, are all carried day and night on the Rhine. The particular characteristics of the river dictated the development of barges and tugboats for a 1000 years and no doubt will continue to do so.

33) Lau van den Wijngaard, skipper and owner of the steam tug *"Gonda"*.

34) Stoomsleepboot *"Fatima"* built in 1929 by the "Holland" shipyard in Hardinxveld. She had a 550 hp steam engine and measured 32.6 by 6.2m.

35) The 1904 steam tug *"Winterswijk"* was converted to diesel power in 1952 with a 250 hp Bolnes diesel engine. Note the distinctive central wheel-house and bridge.

Sleepschepen & Raderschepen

Prior to 1850, the usual maximum size for a Rhine river boat was around 30m. This was mainly due to the constructional techniques inherent in wooden boat-building. It was of course possible to build larger ships, but to build a ship to what essentially would be sea going size and strength, was not economical for a humble river boat. The industrial revolution and availability of good quality iron as a building material changed all that. Simple metalworking skills now allowed basic, cheap, strong and long "barges" to be built. At the same time as the revolution in building material was taking place, steamboats also became commonplace. As we saw in the previous chapter, the Rhine is not a river to be taken lightly. Even today the river pilot warns, *"Above Koblenz navigation requires great care, especially along the dangerous narrows between St. Goar and Bingen. The current is very strong and a pilot is obligatory. Navigation from Koblenz is generally only possible by tow or tugboat, except for high powered vessels"*. Now with powerful steam tugs to pull them, great fleets of huge barges were built. These were substantial craft, built along the lines of their French and Belgian counterparts, with comfortable living quarters for the full-time, live-aboard skipper. Initially these were without sailing-rig or motor, but some had a basic mast and squaresail as a back-up. Traditionally all the river ships on the Rhine, Kempenaar, spits, klipper or whatever, have always been lumped together in the Netherlands as Rijnaken. This goes back to the time when the predominant river ship was the two masted Dorstense aak built in the German town of Dorstens. Most non-marine Dutch dictionaries simply define the word "aak" as barge. Inside this all enveloping Rijnaken umbrella, any ship without either sails or motor was referred to as a "kast". Kast, meaning cupboard or chest, is also the Dutch word for a dumb- barge or lighter. Where these were pulled by tugboats, known as "sleepboten", they were called "sleepschepen". After the first world war, as marine diesel engines became more widely available, some skippers, yearning to be independent, converted their ships to "motorsleepschepen". They could use their relatively low powered motors on the lower reaches of the great rivers, but upstream on the Rhine, with a current of maybe 6 knots or more, the mighty paddle-wheel steam tugs were still needed to help the motorsleepschepen complete their journey. These very impressive river tugs came in all shapes and sizes. The basic two types however, were a single-engined ship with a steam engine driving a screw propeller and larger ships with up to 4 engines turning two paddle-wheels amidships. These paddle-wheel ships were called "Radersleepboten". Up to 75m long, with a beam of 20m over the paddles, they could produce a healthy 1500 hp. Much of the trade on the Rhine was the transport of coal from Germany. This was what the steamboats ran on and so it was economically viable for these ships to carry on working well into the 1950's, before being usurped by diesel engined tugs. At this time, after the second world war, even larger numbers of sleepschepen adopted motors. The size of the ships also grew and any semblance of ship-like beauty that had lingered on was sacrificed to pure functionality.

In 1937 the records show that 27,669 motorschepen passed through Tolkamer, the customs post on the Rhine, on the border between the Netherlands and Germany.

Compare this to the much greater number of sleep and zeilschepen, 78,989, passing through in the same year. In 1975 the sleepvaart trade had dropped to 37,808 and the number of passing motorschepen had risen to 170,447.

36) The Raderboot "Ad Linden VI". These shallow draft, paddle-wheel steam tugs had ample power to pull strings of barges up the Rhine against the strong current. Good reserves of coal in Germany ensured that they kept going right up until the late 1950's.

CHAPTER SEVEN

Spits types

The spits has one of the longest histories of all the binnenvaart ships. The first built of wood and pulled by horses and the last made from steel with powerful diesel engines. In the intervening years, unlike many other inland freight ships, they did not pass through the sailing-barge stage. Why was this and how exactly did the spits evolve? The spitsen family tree is extremely large and varied, but it is well worth attempting to unravel the modern spits ancestry.

Ships bearing the name spits were being built in the early part of the nineteenth century and the spits as we know it today was still being built in 1970. In the same way that the title of tjalk generically covers a whole host of different ship derivations, all with something in common, so too does the title spits. The strange thing is, that although the Dutch word of spits means "pointed", virtually all the spitsen built were extremely blunt in hull form and anything but pointed.

The name first appeared on a relatively small type of ship, built in France and Belgium around 1810-1820. These were more or less rectangular in form, with a bow more reminiscent of a Dutch sailing-barge, such as the tjalk or aak. To conform with the locks in their areas of operation they had a maximum beam of 4.9m and a length between 20-30m. This form was sharper than was usual for cargo ships built in these regions at this time, and so in France they were called "pointu" and in Belgium "spits". They were not built in any great number as the twentieth century dawned, but those that were built now had a common size of 38.5 by 5.05m. The reasons for this change in size lie with the French government and a gentleman named Charles de Saulces de Freycinet. He was the French minister of public works from 1877 to 1879 and his mission was to standardize all the French locks and navigational waterways. Taking many factors into account, including existing ship and lock size, de Freycinet came up with a French standard of 40m by 5.2m for locks and a minimal navigational depth of 1.8m on all standardized waterways. These standards exist today and are commonly referred to as "Freycinet size".

The French, Belgian and Dutch canal network was of course very well established long before de Freycinet came onto the scene. The ships in any particular region were built to a size that was practical for their area of operation. In Belgium and northern France the larger locks could all take ships of 40m by 5m and consequently this was the size the ships were already built to conform with.

Walenschepen

The ships that most resemble the modern day spits were angular in shape, built of wood, with a greatest size of 38m by 5m and first appeared in large numbers in the early nineteenth century. They were built mostly in the southern part of the low countries, in the area that would eventually become what we recognize today as Belgium and northern France. In 1840 the Walloon speaking region of the Netherlands became Belgium. The large canal barges built here were called Walenschepen, or Walenpont, on account of this.

The French navigational rivers all had strong currents and the smaller rivers and canals tended to be tree lined with narrow tow-paths. This made sailing impractical and so, unlike the waters farther north in the Netherlands, the sailing-barge did not prosper here.

The ships were mostly pulled by the crew in the case of smaller ships, but with the larger Walenschepen, horses or mules were needed. A small mast was set about two-thirds of the way along the ship and on the occasions that the wind blew along the canal from astern, a square-sail, hoisted on a yard, but canted a little upwards, looking something like a lug-sail, was pressed into use. This was called an "emerzeil". It was small in relation to the size of the ship that carried it and it never grew to the proportions seen across the channel on the English Humber keels for example, which were built during the same period.

From around 1850, all ships built in Belgium and France to the size of what would later become "Freycinet" dimensions, were referred to by the Belgians as "spitsen". The Dutch speaking skippers said that their French speaking colleagues had "une peniche Flamande" and the French eventually came to call them "bateau Freycinet". Call them what you will, it is fair to say that these ships were the true ancestors of the modern day spits.

37) A wooden Walenschip with skipper, family and horsepower.

The Doornikker / Peniche

These Walenschepen were built in several different variations. The most numerous came from the regions around Doornik and Penis, close to the French border, on the Belgian Schelde. In France these became Peniches and in Belgium, Doornikkers. They had a size of 37-39 by 5 by 1.8m. This gave a capacity of around 290 tons. The even larger ships, which travelled only on the rivers, were deeper in draft and loaded nearer 370 tons. This was a not inconsiderable load for those times. The Doornikker was of angular build, bluff bowed, with a bold stempost and a pronounced rubbing strake at bow and stern only. It had virtually no sheer, with a small rise appearing only on the bow. The bow had a small inward curve above the rubbing strake and a distinctive white timber across the stem forming a cross with the stempost. This feature was the hallmark of a true Doornikker. The rudder was wooden and mounted on the sternpost on conventional gudgeons and pintles. It was a very large piece of equipment, up to 4.5m long in the horizontal plane. Because of this extreme length, the rearward section was pivoted to allow it to be swung upwards in harbour, to lie vertically flush with the rest of the rudder. This was sometimes called a "roer-zwaard" (rudder lee-board) and indeed the lift-up section looks and functions much like a lee-board. To successfully operate a rudder of this length a very long tiller was also needed. The Doornikker tiller was constructed in two sections. The first, and heaviest, section was rigidly fixed to the rudder head and the second, folding part, was positioned on top of the first section, held in place by a metal stirrup and clamp. When a Doornikker was in a lock, the roer-zwaard was lifted, the tiller folded back and the whole arrangement could now lie flat against the stern of the ship. In this way the ship would fit exactly into the lock, with absolutely no room to spare. The hatch-boards were generally flat, but occasionally had a little curve built into them. At the midpoint of the ship the cargo space was split into two parts by a deckhouse or "roef". In fact, this was used to house the ships motive power, the horses or mules. This was a fine, airy stable for them and this roef became known as the "paardenroef". When the horse was replaced by steam tugs at the turn of the century, many skippers moved into the paardenroef and made a far more pleasing home for themselves. Ships built at this time often had a purpose-built skipper's quarter where the paardenroef used to be and although far more luxurious it still kept its former name.

However, when a horse or two were still carried, the skipper, his wife and sometimes the crewman all lived together in the area at the stern of the ship, under the cockpit, in the space called the "achteronder". The skippers took great care of their horses in the same way that later skippers cared for their engines. In both cases a sick "engine" was no good at all and meant a loss of earnings. The horses and mules were specially trained for their work, they had to be of a steady disposition, not prone to bolting or excitable actions and be able to work steadily all day. Of course the same could be said of the skipper and in the same way that not all men are suited to be the master of a ship, not all horses are suited to the work. In winter especially, a canal-side farmer was often pleased to hire his plough horses out to passing ships. They were not trained for the task however and sadly many were drowned when things got out of hand.

The Balland

Another version of the Walenschip was the Ballant or Challand. This was also a word used for a dumb barge or lighter. The Balland looked much like a Doornikker, but was plumper, less angular, generally more rounded and the stempost was straight, with no inward falling top-section. They carried a small mast and paardenroef like the Doornikker and were in most aspects very similar. They were all built to spits size.

The various versions of the wooden Walenschip were hugely successful. They traded all over northern Europe to France, Belgium, the Netherlands, Germany, Luxembourg and Switzerland. Coal, sand, gravel, stone, iron ore, lumber, mining supplies and farm produce, all were carried by the ubiquitous Walenschepen. They continued to be built in wooden form right up to 1920, some even as true motor-ships with an inboard engine.

The Baquet de Charleroi, or The "Half Spits"

Before we come to the iron and steel ships that are today commonly called spitsen, there is one other ship that is worth noting. Although not built to spits measurements, these little ships do look a little like a scaled down version of their bigger brothers. The canal that linked Brussels to Charleroi opened in 1832. Unlike the flat lands of the Netherlands the countryside in this region is decidedly hilly. The canal was 75 kilometres in length with 55 locks to negotiate, all of them rather small. At Ronquieres alone there was a flight of 15. Progress was slow and a typical transit took 21 hours. The Baquet was built to a size of only 19.2 by 2.9m, this enabled them to fit into the locks diagonally and completely fill them. They were originally of wooden construction and looked a little more like sailing-barges than their lumbering horse-drawn brothers. They had a distinctive inward-falling topside above the rubbing-strake, which in turn was full and distinctly fat at bow and stern, similar to the stuizen found on a tjalk. Indeed to compound the comparison, some were even seen away from their home canal on more open waters, with full sailing-rig and lee-boards. Later versions were built in iron and towards the end of their life in 1930, even in ferro-cement. The end came in 1932 when the Brussels to Charleroi canal was opened up to larger ships. The Baquet had had its day, however many were lengthened, fitted with motors or did service as house boats. There are still a few to be spotted today by the eagle-eyed observer.

Ship-lifts

As mentioned earlier, at Ronquieres, on the Canal Brussels-Charleroi, it had been necessary to build a flight of 15 locks to raise the level of the canal high enough to continue navigating to Brussels. After world war II, the density of traffic and more importantly the sheer physical size of the ships, grew rapidly. On April 1st 1968, the locks at Ronquieres were bypassed by a ship-lift.This was basically a huge "bath tub" of water into which the barge was sailed. This tub, mounted on 236 wheels, was then pulled up a one and a half kilometre long incline and so raised almost 70m in one go. The bath, 91m by 12m, could take ships up to a massive 1350 tons. Electrical power, coupled with a cunning counterweight system, made for a very efficient lift. Time for transit was cut by a third, from 21 to 14 hours.

A similar geographical problem was encountered a little to the west, on the route between the Canal Brussels-Charleroi and Mons. This is a canal of only 19 kilometres, but with a vertical rise of 80m. As early as 1884 a system of 4 hydraulic ship-lifts was installed, each with a vertical lift of 17m. In 1964 work started on a single new lift that would eventually raise barges of up to 1350 tons through the 73m in one go.

The Spits

Around 1870, the first Walenschepen, built to Freycinet dimensions and constructed from iron, appeared. These were never known as anything except spitsen and in 100 years of constructional life, during which time literally tens of thousands were built, they hardly changed their form at all.

When iron found its way into the shipyards of the binnenvaart, it first found favour with the builders of the huge dumb barges, the "kasten". It was not long, however, before the builders of spitsen also saw its' worth and the spits was soon being built in iron, alongside its wooden counterparts.

Some were built with an iron hull and a wooden bottom, as wood was accepted as easier to repair and renew than a riveted· iron bottom. These composite ships were called "mixte" ships. By 1900 very few wooden spitsen were being constructed and steel soon superseded iron, although riveting, as opposed to welding, was still the method used to fasten the plates together. In later years, after the second world war, when electric welding became available, the size, shape and form of the spits changed dramatically.

The first iron ships looked much like the long, plump, Walenschepen from which they had descended. They even retained the paardenroef midway along the hold, although this was now almost exclusively used by the skipper. In fact, even the very first purpose-built motorspits, with a 50 hp motor, still featured a "cabine centrale". They were still occasionally pulled by horses, but mostly by this time they used the assistance of a "sleepboot" (tugboat).

The early spitsen were steered from an open cockpit situated on the extreme stern of the ship. A very large wooden rudder, with a lifting after-section, was in turn married to a two-piece wooden tiller. The helmsman was provided with iron strips riveted to the deck, to allow him to find grip on the sometimes slippery and wet deck. Gradually the wooden rudder and tiller was replaced by items made from iron and eventually, as inboard motors arrived on the scene, a horizontally mounted wheel still fitted in an open cockpit, became standard practice. A small mast with hulptuig was carried. Unlike their sailing counterparts, the spits often appeared with curved rather than flat hatch-boards.This was due to the profusion of Poplar wood available in Belgium and northern France. Poplar wood gave relatively small planks and these when built into hatch-boards allowed a curved board to be built. This gave a little extra storage space and also allowed water to be easily shed. These became known as "Friese luiken".

Although the spits was now built to a more or less common Freycinet size, different building regions continued to build slightly different spitsen.

Samberspits

By the early part of this century, on the larger rivers and canals, locks even larger than Freycinet size were being constructed. In the Samber region of Belgium, the river Samber provides the vital link between the river Seine (and Paris) in France and Brussels, via the Canal Brussels-Charleroi. This link with France and the nature of the river Samber, conspired to produce a new, larger spits to come into being, the "Samberspits". These ships were built in iron to a new common size of 47m, 8.5m longer than a "conventional" spits. This allowed a capacity of 420-470 tons. The bow and new, longer hull were those of a spits in all respects, but they now had a counter-stern, with a stern hung, semi-balanced, iron rudder. The cockpit was still at the stern, but the new rudder allowed the helmsman to be moved a little farther forward and a horizontal wheel to be fitted. At this time and on these ships, a rudimentary open-sided wheel-house first began to appear. These ships looked very much like their distant cousins, the Dutch sailing zeilkast (see chapter 4). Although the space under the cockpit, the "achteronder" was still used for sleeping, the shape of the hull and the increasing use of inboard motors made it necessary to incorporate additional accommodation. Often the "cabine centrale" was still used, but it became the normal practice to build a cabin (the roef) forward of the helmsman's position. This had always been the way on the Dutch sailing-barge fleet and this type of roef was known as a "zeilroef".

Maasspits

Nijmegen is a frontier town, where a barge skipper can head east into Germany, west into the Netherlands, or navigate the river Maas to the most southern city of the Netherlands, Maastricht. In fact, much of the Maas in Limburg is by-passed by the Juliana Kanaal, but the water-route continues into Belgium, joining the Meuse at Luik and then on to the Samber at Namen. The Limburgse Maas forms a vital link in the waterways network. The river Maas is a powerful river and the ships that navigated it developed a different hull shape to cope with the strong flow. The early Maasspitsen, built of wood, had a right angled chine on a rather straight hull, but with a distinctive bow and stern. The later iron ships were sometimes still built this way, but others developed a rounded bilge. These later ships are more streamlined, something a conventional spits could never be accused of. The hull has a more exaggerated sheer in its forward and after section than other spitsen, with a pointed bow, although still not as sharp as the lovely stem found on one of its contemporaries, the river klipper. The stern was full and rounded, but in common with the bow it was just a little sharper to aid the water flow around it. These ships retained the large spits wooden rudder and tiller, but, as was the practice with Dutch ships, they often incorporated a decorated and carved wooden ornament, called the "klik", into the construction. This would mostly carry a stylized illustration of the cornucopia (the horn of plenty), along with the ships and/or skipper's name and town of origin.

38) In 1940 many of the canals in the Netherlands were dry as a result of bombing. Due to this, many ships were left high and dry and in some cases suffered damage. In this case, the Maasspits *"Rodolfa"* suffered only a broken rudder. With this repaired and when the water was restored, skipper H. Blijen (pictured on deck) continued in his trade. Note the ship's flat bottom and two-piece tiller.

39) The Dutch built Kempenaar *"Willem"*, a 463 ton ship built in 1907 at the "Boot" shipyard in Leiderdorp.

The smallest lock on the Maas at the turn of the century measured 45m in length and so the Maasspits was generally built to around 42-43m, giving a carrying capacity of 380-420 tons. They were seldom built with a central roef, instead as they were really quite large ships, the achteronder still provided enough living space. When inboard engines arrived, evicting the skipper from the achteronder, a zeilroef had to be built to house the skipper.

Herna, Mignolle & Spitsbek

Another spits, built on and around the river Maas, was the wooden Herna. This was a variant of the virtually identical Mignolle or Spitsbek. However, only the Herna survived in iron form into the twentieth century. With a spits bow and hull shape forward, the stern is unmistakable. Instead of the plates being drawn together in a pleasing rounded shape, the bottom plates of the Herna continue in a flat curve from the keel upwards. This gives a not particularly pleasing, but functional, flat, after-section. From this is hung a semi-balanced iron rudder. They were built to traditional spits dimensions of 38.5 by 5m.

The Motorspits evolves

At the turn of the century steam was a common form of propulsion for tugboats on the great rivers and increasingly so on the smaller rivers and canals. Slowly but surely, the horse was being replaced as a barge's motive power by the internal combustion engine. By 1920 the way forward was clear and most new spitsen were built as motor-ships, whilst others were rapidly converting to small inboard installations, or single and multiple zijschroef arrangements (see chapter 2).

Beurtmotors (small motor-ships) were being built as early as 1900; by 1920 the all new, purpose-built motor-ship, the "luxemotor", had appeared on the scene. It was time to modernize spits building and develop the "perfect spits". This ship had of course to be efficiently motorized and the full round stern of the spits was not ideal for this purpose. In the same way that the hull form of the sailing tjalken and aken made the retro-fitting of motors difficult, the stern of the spits would have to change. Some skippers got around the problem by using multiple zijschroef installations, but this was far from ideal and decidedly primitive compared to the luxemotor.

First attempts used the achteronder as an engine-room, with a tail-shaft fitted on one side of the rudder to give a "wing" engine. This worked fairly well, but was still not truly effective. The goal was to achieve a centre line propeller. This line of thought led to several different attempts to achieve the goal. One interesting idea was to fit a central shaft tunnel and conventional shaft, but where one would, under normal circumstances, expect the propeller to be located, is instead a universal joint, leading to a short shaft terminating in a propeller at the outboard edge of the rudder, which in turn is cut away to accept it. The rudder also has a hanging bracket with a bearing to support the shaft. This arrangement meant that as the rudder turned, the direction of thrust of the propeller also turned. Acting almost like a modern outboard motor, a degree of extra manoeuverability was introduced. However, if you think about it, it will be apparent that with this set up there is no flow of water over the rudder except in astern, so when going ahead the rudder is not functioning to its best effect. The answer was to add an extension to the trailing edge of the rudder, so that the generated water-flow when in forward propulsion could be utilized. By making this section independently articulated, a fine degree of tuning could be achieved.

However, all this engineering work was intensely vulnerable to damage and however good this might have been in competent hands it was not the way forward. More conventional designs had to be considered.

The first really successful retro-fitted iron spitsen had a tunnel built into the centre line of the stern and a cutaway rudder. On brand new ships, "nagelnieuw" as the Dutch would say, an alternative stern shape was designed. The true motorspits stern retains the full rounded portion above the empty waterline, but then has a slight counter, sometimes with a small skeg and a central propeller. The rudder, with a constant stream of fast moving water being directed over it, no longer needed to be of the massive size seen previously. The lifting after section was deleted and a smaller streamlined iron version substituted.

When hydraulic pumps and machinery became available, more and more spitsen were converted to twin, hydraulically powered rudders, with the propeller situated on the centre line in-between. This shape was to remain right up to the end of the spitsen building life. The hull however evolved into two slightly different types. A ship built with a hard chine between bottom and side would float higher and draw less water than those ships with a rounded bilge shape. This was an advantage in many ways, but the down side was that due to the shallow draft, an empty spits with a hard chine would behave like a leaf on a pond. The propeller being close to the surface would suck in air and cavitate, providing greatly reduced performance. A round-bilged ship would still be a handful when sailed empty, but with more immersed area, it was at least manageable.

Natte & Droge Spitsen

This problem resulted in the so-called "natte spitsen" and the "droge spitsen". The wet and the dry spitsen. Simply, this meant that a "natte spits" would have a watertight area in the cargo space, about one metre high, as far aft as possible and isolated from the rest of the hold. This was able to be flooded with canal or river water, allowing the ship, especially the after section, to sink a little lower in the water to make it more manageable. This little feature was also used to negotiate the occasional low bridge. Of course this space had to be thoroughly dry before a cargo could be carried in it once more. As most ships seem to rot from the inside out, a "natte spits" should be examined carefully in the wet-hold area before purchase.

Nederlandse & Belgische Spitsen

The "cabine centrale" was also considered old-fashioned and since it got in the way of the new mechanical loading machinery, it had to go. With the central roef gone and the achteronder full of machinery, an alternative living space had to be designed. This came in two main forms. The first was favoured by the Belgian skippers and took the form of a "zeilroef" forward of the wheel-house, which was itself of substantial construction and formed part of the living space. The wheel-house was situated towards the stern of the ship, over the engine-room. Although every ship was (and still is), unique, built to the owners preferences, a more or less standard type structure evolved. Typically, a Belgian spits would have a comfortable wheel-house, in essence an integral part of the living space, with access from here directly into the saloon or roef. Here would be the dining table and chairs and a coal burning stove. Forward of this and down a step or two would be the sleeping area, with perhaps a couple of comfortable bedsteads in a curtained off part of the room. Forward of here and not normally accessible from the living area, was the cargo space. Behind the wheel-house, almost at the extreme end of the ship, was the so-called "theehut".

This was simply a small self-contained cooking space, where the skipper and crew could sit for coffee and a cigarette, without intruding into the main part of the accommodation. The second of the two accommodation types was favoured by the Dutch skippers and was, not surprisingly, similar to that found on the luxemotor. This used the upper part of the achteronder of the ship, built up above deck level to form a "salon roef". Forward of this was the wheel-house, which again formed an integral part of the accommodation area. From the comfortable wheel-house a companionway, always on the port side, led down aft to the "salonroef". This formed the main living and dining area. To port and starboard would be found a galley and washroom respectively and located right aft would be the sleeping space. This often had two portholes in its aft facing wall. Many variations on these two basic types were of course built, reflecting the individuality of the skippers and their wives! Some disliked sleeping over the engine-room; some preferred an engine right aft with a short shaft and some found an engine further forward allowed a larger engine-room which was easier to work in. Some even had a combination of both types, with accommodation both before and after the wheel-house. Be that as it may, the typical Belgian spits and the typical Dutch spits came into being and are still easily identified.

"Vasco", built in 1952 and now in use as a houseboat and art studio in Gouda, is a good example of a Belgian spits, with an aft wheel-house and remnants of a "theehut" behind it. *"Vasco"*, a "natte" spits bought straight out of trade, is still in good working order with an American, General Motors engine from a Sherman tank. At the other end of the ship, on the fore-deck, is a power driven mechanical winch used to recover the twin anchors and for manoeuvreing the ship in harbour with warping drums. A stern anchor with its own hawse hole was also standard to all spits types. A davit is also located here, used to haul the anchors inboard when necessary. Down below the fore-deck, in the "vooronder", is a separate living space for the deck-hand.

The whole anchoring, manoeuvreing and loading operation became motorized at the same time as the spits was becoming a modern motor-ship. Down below the fore-deck, or in a separate self-contained space on deck, was a generator set. Early versions used a small petrol or diesel engine to provide power to the anchor winch. As time progressed, reliable electrical power became available for the ship's accommodation and other ship-systems such as deck washing and mechanical loading devices.

The Spits grows again

When the Canal du Nord was completed, with huge locks that had dimensions of 92 by 6m, the spits, never a ship to lag behind progress, grew again. These ships were called not altogether surprisingly, Canal Du Nord spitsen. They had a common dimension of 45-55 by 5.7m. They could of course have been bigger; the technology of the time allowed it, but then the canals of northern France would have been denied to them. The way around this was simply to make use of the "koppelverband", a system already in use on the great rivers for manoeuvreing lighters. This was simply a coupling device that allowed one ship to push another from behind, or for both to use their engines if necessary. Two 45 metre Canal Du Nord spitsen, coupled in this way, filled a lock very nicely.

By 1950, the spits was the most numerous and popular binnenvaart ship in the Netherlands. "Wij varen internationaal" (we trade internationally) was their catch-phrase. The luxemotor, that had been the cutting edge of motor-ship evolution, was no longer in production and although many were lengthened, along with their older ex-sailing counterparts, they could not compete with the sheer brute size and strength of the spits. Not content with outgrowing all its rivals, the spits went on in the 1980's to become the "Super-Spits".

These were built to uncompromising Canal du Nord dimensions and were now over 70m long carrying 900 tons of cargo. Many had twin-engines of more than 1000 hp each and a third in the bow to aid manoeuvreing. But even these ships were to become dwarfed by those that were to follow in the late twentieth century.

40) The Kempenspits *"Jacoba"* in Maassluis. The bow is more rounded and built from more plates than a conventional spits.

Kempenaar / Kempenspits

Before the opening of the Albertkanaal in 1930, ships wishing to reach Antwerpen from inland had to travel on the Kempenkanaal. The locks on this canal had dimensions of 50 by 6.8m. Ships built to fit into this size of lock and using this route became known as Kempenaars.

The draft of the ship was also very important. The Zuid-Willemsvaart was part of the Kempenaar's route, running from the Juliana Kanaal in Maastricht, in a northerly loop, through to Antwerpen. On the Zuid-Willemsvaart the maximum depth available was 1.9m. This meant that a sturdy ship, built in a yard such as "Driesens" in Weert, could load only 440 tons before the maximum draft was reached. At this stage she would not be full, in fact a "Driesens" built Kempenaar could load an impressive 593 tons when loaded to capacity. A more rounded and lightly built ship on the other hand, like many of those built in Maasstricht, could load more than 460 tons and still draw less than the 1.9m allowable. What was the most important, strength of ship, or weight of cargo? You paid your money and took your choice.

The first Kempenaars were built during the last years of the nineteenth century, almost exclusively in iron and were in many respects similar to spitsen. In fact, ships that anywhere else would be called spitsen, were called Kempenaars simply because of their area of operation and specific dimensions peculiar to the Kempenkanaal. These Kempenspitsen as they became known, tended to be built with Friese-luiken and a bow shape similar to the Maasspits, but with a slightly sharper stem. This was to allow more efficient operation on the rivers and open water around Antwerpen. In Belgium they acquired the name of "Fox", as in Fox-terrier, which is rather surprising for a 50 metre ship loading up to 700 tons!

The true Kempenaar, as distinct from a Kempenspits, had a different hull form. The stern was that of a Samberspits, with a distinct counter and semi-balanced spade rudder. At the bow, the more typical river-ship, or Maasspits type of sharp stem was to be found. On deck, above the overhanging stern, was the "stuurstand" (a partially enclosed steering position) with a horizontal wheel driving the rudder by means of a quadrant and toothed wheel. Forward of the steering position was a low zeilroef in which the skipper made his home. About half-way along the ship's length was a small mast from which an emerzeil could be flown. When horses and a jaaglijn were used, the line ran through an eye at the masthead to a strong point aft.

By 1920, along with the spits, the Kempenaar was being forced by necessity to evolve into a motor-ship. Many of the larger ships were simply lengthened farther and kept as sleepschepen or lighters. Unlike many of the English lighters, or dumb-barges, these ships had names and provided a full time home for proud, hard working families. The mere fact that they had to rely on tug-boats made no difference to their outlook. It was what their fathers and grandfathers had done before them. In this way, the Kempenaar grew to a size that is no longer of real relevance to this book. Along with the Super-Spits they became too large for either house-boats or private cruising homes. Motorkempenaars were built in the same manner as motorspitsen and underwent the same process of evolution, involving one or more zijschroef installations and eventually inboard diesel engines.

A typical post-second world war Kempenaar or Kempenspits would be 50m long, 6.5m in the beam and fitted with an inboard diesel engine of between 60-100 hp. On deck the open steering place had gone, to be replaced by a purpose-built wheel-house. Forward of this, in typical Belgian fashion, was the familiar zeilroef, although in most cases it had now grown upwards and forwards. A small mast was still carried, but on almost all the Kempenaars this was now located forward of the hatches on the fore-deck, leaving the hold area clear for loading and unloading.

"Modern" Kempenaar

At the end of the 1950's and beginning of the 1960's a new Kempenaar appeared. Surprisingly, it was not as might be expected a larger ship, but instead it was built to original Kempenaar dimensions. They carried less cargo than their older cousins, 500 instead of 700 tons, but they could deliver their load faster and more efficiently. The new Kempenaar was built with a streamlined hull form, a sharp bow and overhanging counter-stern. They could still use the smaller waterways denied to their bigger brothers and using modern engines, coupled to their new "slippery" shape, they were actually more fuel efficient. The one big feature that sets them apart from their ancestors is, that without exception, the new Kempenaars were built with a luxemotor type forward wheel-house and attached behind this, a salonroef. A new Kempenaar can easily be mistaken for a luxemotor, but the counter-stern has no tumblehome, the bow is sharper, not quite so straight, and has a slight, but distinctive, concave top-section.

Dortmunders etc.

In the western part of Germany, there is a route to the sea that does not involve crossing the frontier into the Netherlands. On the Rhein below Dusseldorf, at Duisburg, the Rhein-Herne kanal runs for 29 miles (46k) to Henrichenburg. Here it connects with the Dortmund-Ems kanal and after a 165 mile (266k) run, gains access to the North Sea through the Ems estuary and the Waddenzee. As in other regions, special ships evolved for this particular route. It is unlikely that any of these ships will be adopted for private use, certainly their beam makes them unsuitable for "normal" canal use, but their size at the smallest end of the range and certainly at the present time their price, makes their inclusion worthwhile. The Dortmunder is a large, relatively modern (i.e. post-luxemotor) motor-ship, built for the Dortmund-Ems kanal. They are very coaster-like and their sea-keeping abilities may render them attractive to some people. The common size for a Dortmunder was 67 by 8.20m. Another similar type, and the biggest that I intend to mention, is the Rijn-Hernekanaalschip. With similar features to the Dortmunder, they had a common size of 80 by 9.5m.

note: kanal = German spelling
kanaal = Dutch spelling
canal = French & English spelling

41) A small beurtmotorboot. Many of these ships retained an open steering position, but this example has been fitted with a "pillar-box" wheel-house. Note the curved structure of the motor-roef forward of the wheel-house.

42) The motorbeurtschip *"Wilhelmina"*, built in 1934, worked in the Maastricht area under her skipper Bartje Bok. His father owned the sleepspits *"Corona"*, seen in the background and with *"Wilhelmina"* towing from in front, father and son worked together.

CHAPTER EIGHT

Beurtschepen & Luxemotors

Motor-ships, in the form of steamboats, had been seen on and around the waterways and harbours of the Netherlands since the 1850's. They served many functions, but due to the space taken up by the steam engine itself, the boiler and the coal bunkers, their main service was to provide power to pull and push other ships, rather than to carry cargo of their own. In 1890, in Germany, Carl Benz made the first serious attempts to build a relatively small marine internal combustion engine. Two years later, Rudolph Diesel produced the new type of compression ignition engine that to this day bears his name. In the Netherlands, Jan Brons built his first successful marine diesel engine in 1897. His target market was the "beurtvaart". Before lorries and roads made a virtual monopoly of the distribution of goods, this trade was handled by the "regular" ships of the "beurtvaart". These were small sailing-ships, which, because of their dimensions, could penetrate deep into the countryside, using the small drainage ditches and canals. The method of propulsion was by sailing, or more often pulling, or poling with a long pole known as a "vaarboom". They carried butter, vegetables, household goods, gossip and news. They prided themselves on maintaining a regular service to their customers. It didn't take much for Jan Brons and the "beurtschippers" to see the advantages of an engine. The first "motorbeurtschepen" appeared in the first years of the twentieth century. Starting with ships of around 15m in length, carrying 30 tons or so, in some areas they quickly grew to 40m in length, with a capacity of up to 250 tons. The hull form of these larger ships was that of the luxemotor, but of course they pre-dated it by some twenty years. The beurtmotor has a straight-sided hull for only the middle third of its length. Towards the bow the hull sides curve inwards in a pleasing, flowing manner, to form a straight stem of the type found on many steamboats and river ships. Towards the stern, the hull sides flow around and under, to form a counter. A very distinctive, wide, rubbing-strake (berghout) runs from the top of the counter, horizontally along the ship's side, running parallel to the top of the bulwarks and finishing at the stem. The area of ship's side above the berghout (the boeisel), is a typically Dutch feature. At the rear of the ship, the boeisel falls inwards at an angle of about 45 degrees, to form the typical beurtschip stern. In the first ships, a mast and full sailing-rig was carried in standard sailing-barge fashion, at about two-thirds of the way down the ship's length. In this phase we can see the transition from sail-power to motor-power, with pure nineteenth century sailing-rig technology married to twentieth century fossil-fuel dependence. As time progressed and faith in the diesel engine grew, the mast became purely a loading crane and the boom formed the derrick. The boom was operated by hand, by means of a manual mechanical winch at the foot of the mast. Later ships employed a small petrol or diesel engine on the fore-deck to serve this purpose. In common with most binnenvaart ships of this period, the mast was soon moved forward to allow easy access to the cargo hold. Unlike the large spitsen or Kempenaars, the hold of a beurtschip was relatively narrow, with disproportionately wide side-decks. This was to allow the crew to load and unload small amounts of cargo, in, more often than not, less than perfect conditions. The small opening to the hold also had the benefit, in many cases, of being able to dispense with the more normal central beam (scheerboom), supporting two rows of hatches. Instead, a single row of flat hatch-boards could be used.

43) Rotterdamse Coolhaven, the home of the beurtvaarder between the wars. Note the chap in the foreground taking a crafty rest in the shade of the pallets.

The first beurtmotors had a horizontal wheel in an open cockpit which soon gave way to a vertically mounted wheel and a small steering hut. Forward of the steering hut was a small skylight, or perhaps a zeilroef, but with one important difference; if you lift the hatch and look in here you will not find the elegant mahogany interior of the skipper's home. No, in here is the ship's heart, the motor. One of the most common ship's engines of the time was the "Liggende Renes". This was a single-cylinder engine with a barrel like a steam engine and two huge external spoked flywheels looking like those of a gun carriage. Others made by Kromhout and Brons were also popular. Although horsepower was relatively low, the heavy flywheels and slow-revving motors gave tremendous reliable torque. These ships served the purpose of the lorries that were to supersede them and like the lorries they had no need to provide a permanent home for the driver. The skipper and crew of a beurtschip were expected to make a temporary home for themselves under the fore-deck, in the "vooronder".

1900 to 1930 were the golden years for the beurtschip. The Coolhaven in Rotterdam and the Schie in Delfshaven were homes to vast fleets of beurtvaarders, some big, some small, but all busy carrying the manufactured goods of the cities to the countryside and the produce of the countryside back to the cities. Many variations on the basic theme were built to suit particular circumstances.

At the end of the nineteenth century, in the farming area around Beverwijk, which lies to the east of Amsterdam, a co-operative of farmers worked with the captain of a steamboat to provide a regular flow of farm produce to the markets of Amsterdam. This proved to be a very successful co-operation and when the steamboat became too old to continue, it was decided to build a new motor-ship specifically for this trade. In 1929, the beurt-vrachtmotorboot "Vereeniging" (meaning union or unity) was built in Spaarndam. For over 30 years "Vereeniging" carried vegetables and other produce, on a daily basis, between Beverwijk and the market in the Marnixstraat in Amsterdam. This was a reasonably large ship by beurtschip standards, measuring 23.84m by 4.36m. With a loaded draft of 1.7m she could carry 56 tons. She was built to make the daily trip from country to town and back again in all seasons and in all weathers. The canals in the area were particularly prone to freezing as they were fairly shallow and the water had no current to keep it moving. "Vereeniging" had a hull built from 7 millimetre steel all round and a special half-round bar was fixed to the bow at the waterline to break the ice and protect the hull from damage by ice splinters. In typical beurtschip style, a heavy berghout was carried all around the ship. This berghout was of particularly stout construction, being of oak and 10 by 10cm in section. As mentioned earlier, most beurtschepen were used in the same way as lorries are today, with no need for full time live-aboard accommodation. "Vereeniging" was one of these, almost always returning to her home base at nights. On the occasions that she was unable to return home, basic short-term living accommodation was provided. In the engine-room, beneath the open steering position, was a small stove and a bunk for the crewman. At the other end of the ship, in the vooronder, was additional living space designed for the occasional carriage of passengers, or for the skipper to stay in whilst away from home. By the time that "Vereeniging" was built, in 1929, diesel engines were becoming more powerful and reliable. She was fitted with a Kromhout, single-cylinder, gloeikop engine, developing some 50 hp. Driving a four bladed propeller of 1 metre diameter, this allowed her to attain a maximum speed of 13 mph (22 kph). At the forward end of the ship, carried on deck, was an 8 hp Armstrong Siddeley diesel motor, driving the loading winches. The hatch-boards themselves were of steel construction and rigid enough to have no need of either longitudinal or athwartships support.

This, coupled with the strong mast and loading derrick, plus the Armstrong Siddeley diesel, made loading and unloading, if not actually easy, at least a great deal easier than the purely manual operation of previous years.

Today, in 1998, *"Vereeniging"* is undergoing restoration work that will bring her once more to her original condition.

Westlandse Motorboot

By the end of the 1914-18 war, a new generation of relatively small gloeikop motors became available. These were light and compact compared to earlier motors and suited the equally light and compact Westlander very well, although, in common with many sailing-ship hulls, the Westlander stern was not ideal for motorizing. No new Westlanders were built after the first world war, but in 1920 a small motor-ship, built to Westlander dimensions, but with a new hull form appeared. These had a sharper bow and a stern similar to the beurtschip. This was the classic motor-ship stern, a sharply raked counter, with an equally sharply inward falling top section, the boeisel.

Interestingly, the first motor-ships to appear on the English narrow canals in the 1880's, steam powered cargo barges carrying coal, cement and similar heavy cargoes, also had this typical counter-stern and inward falling top section. In this case however they retained the bluff almost tjalk-like bow with a distinctive sheer to the forward sections. The motor-ship theme was continued by having a salon roef aft and a small steering position forward of this. On a true motor-ship the steering position was mostly above the engine-room. The Westlandse motorboot had too shallow a draft to permit this and so forward of the steering position was another small roef dedicated to the engine, the "motor-roef". These ships seldom used a full-size wheel-house, as a shallow air-draft was as important as the water-draft. The engine-room of course took up extra space and so the Westlandse motorboot was generally longer than its sailing predecessors. A mast and boom were still fitted, but now only for loading and unloading purposes.

A typical Westlandse motorboot is the*"Ramen en Kistenfabriek"*, built in 1918 to carry milk in the Westland area. She is still in existence and measures 15.8, by a slim 2.8m. She was built with a Skandia gloeikop engine of 13 hp, which was replaced by a Kromhout 15 hp unit in 1926. The Kromhout remained in use until 1984.

In later years, bigger ships, that were nevertheless small by other standards, continued to trade in this area, although they could not use the small water-ways anymore. In the same way that a special ship evolved in many areas (Hagenaar, skutsje and Katwijker for example), the name Westlander came to be applied to virtually any ship operating in the area once reserved for the specialized craft. Today it is still possible to find ships of 20m by 3.5m referred to as Westlanders.

Beurtschepen came in all shapes and sizes. *"Janna Maria"* carried sugar beet pulp and potatoes in the Zaanstreek area north of Amsterdam; fitted with a Kromhout 14 hp motor she was built in 1922 in Leiden. Her measurements were 19.95 by 3.47m. The motorhagenaar (a type originally designed for the low bridges of Den Haag) named *"Pax"*, was built in Leiderdorp in 1905 with a Rennes gloeikop motor of 20 hp. *"Pax"* had dimensions of 20.15 by 3.65m. Finally, the tankschip *"Tar"*, built in 1926, carrying coal-tar for the firm of van Seumeren, was one of the larger beurtmotors. Measuring 26.75 by 4.7m and loading 80 tons, this ship was fitted with a hefty 60 hp Kromhout.

By 1930 the lorry had displaced many of the smaller beurtschepen with its additional ability to reach even those towns with no water access. It meant that the golden days of the beurtvaarder were numbered. Many of the beurtschepen found a new role in the fishing fleet. Other skippers had already seen the threat that the lorry posed and those far sighted enough had made the transition to bigger ships carrying a larger tonnage of cargo, but still on a "regular" basis.

The idea of the reliability of a beurtschip, with the carrying capacity and skippers accommodation of a spits was natural and so the luxemotor was born.

44) Luxe motorschip *"Hendrika"* built in Groningen to typical heavy specification. Early examples such as this ship often had a fully functioning sailing rig and lee-boards.

45) Two sand-barges on the Rijn. *"Roma"* was built with a 70 hp Appingedammer Brons engine in 1926, *"Spes"* with 70 hp Brons in 1930. The term Appingedammer simply distinguishes between the engines built in Appingedam and those built elsewhere.

Luxemotor

In 1920, the first, large, purpose-built motor-ships appeared. These were based on the lessons learnt from the beurtmotor and had the advantage of not being tied to a particular hull shape, a shape which had, in all probability, evolved to benefit wooden shipbuilding practice, or similar earlier building techniques. The luxemotor could draw on all the modern state of the art technology, with all the modern advantages of the twentieth century built in. The first of these new motor-ships were essentially just larger beurtmotors with a salonroef behind the wheel-house, but the evolution of the beurtmotor had provided the prototype for many new ideas and in the luxemotor they were all brought together. The luxemotor can be conveniently divided into three sections, the cargo carrying and bow section, the engine-room and the accommodation.

Unlike other evolutionary compromises, each section was purpose-built. The hull form embraced accepted practice for a ship that would travel and trade mainly on sheltered water, albeit with the ability to cope with strong flowing rivers and containing sufficiently strong framing to withstand limited exposure to open waters, such as the IJsselmeer and the Schelde. It was constructed of riveted steel plates and frames, which allowed ships of different length to be easily built and to allow extension at a later date if necessary. The first examples had a mast and sailing-rig in conventional sailing-ship position (hulptuig) and this did allow a little down-wind sailing. The disadvantage, as we have seen time and again in this book, was that the presence of the bulky structural "mastdek" supporting the mast and the resultant splitting of the hold into two areas, did not help the cargo handling process. It very soon became common practice to move the mast to a position on the fore-deck of the ship, with a boom of sufficient length to cover the whole cargo bay and a mast of much shorter height than that used for a sailing-rig (hijstuig). The short mast was also easier to lower when passing under bridges. A tall mast, as seen on the true sailing-ships, needed a winch and sheerlegs (bokkepoten) to allow it to be lowered safely. The shorter mast could easily be lowered by means of a winch alone. Most of the booms remained wooden, as because of the length required, a steel boom was prohibitively heavy. The mast could be of steel or wood. Where the two-piece hold was retained, mostly on the longer ships used on the great rivers, the mast developed two booms, one facing forward and one aft to allow both hold areas to be easily worked. The dangers inherent in any manual cargo handling operation must not be underrated. It was not for nothing that this rig gained the sinister title of "the murderer and two witnesses."

The luxemotor was built all over the Netherlands and also, although to a much smaller extent, in Belgium. Here it could actually be said to have appeared as early as 1910, but built along spitsen lines and of lighter construction, it was not a true luxemotor as we know it.

Accepted shipbuilding practice of the time, coupled with the skipper/owners' personal preferences, gradually allowed two slightly differing luxemotors to develop. It is in the shape of the bow and stern that this becomes most apparent. The northern shipyards of Groningen and Friesland had always built strong uncompromising ships, many for use in the sometimes stormy waters of the Baltic. Luxemotors from here have a generally blunt appearance. The bow is still rounded in form, less blunt than a spits, but not as sharp as a typical beurtmotor.

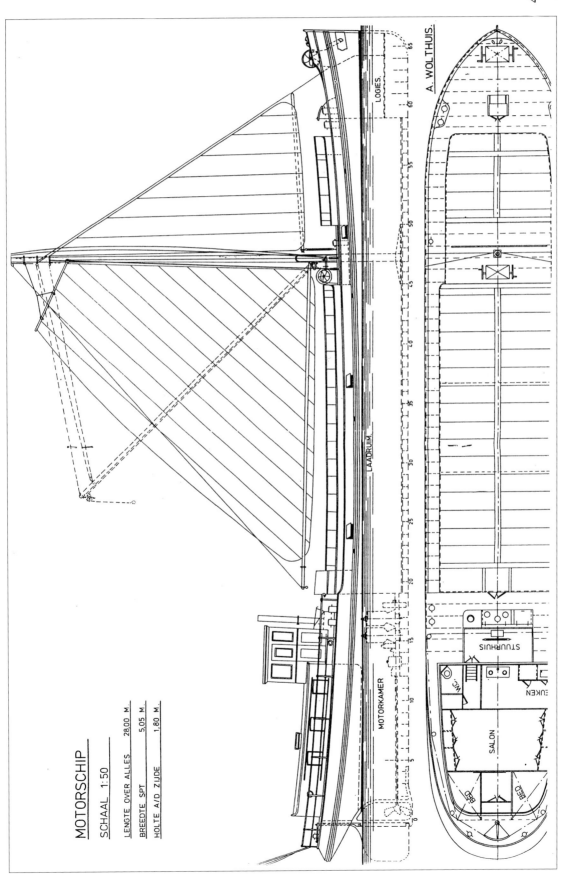

MOTORSCHIP

SCHAAL 1:50

LENGTE OVER ALLES 28.00 M.
BREEDTE SPT   5.05 M.
HOLTE A/D ZIJDE   1,80 M.

LOGIES.

LAADRUIM.

MOTORKAMER.

A. WOLTHUIS.

STUURHUIS

KEUKEN

W.C.

SALON

BED

BED

46) Motorschip.
A Wolthuis.

73

47) Luxemotor "Allegonda", built by Fikkers of Foxhole in 1932. She was fitted with a twin-cylinder Brons engine from new and kept the same engine for 59 years. At this time, after a major seizure due to oil starvation, repairs became uneconomical and a new Scania engine was installed. The owner, B. van der Wal said: "It was a wonderful engine, it stood three metres high and ran at 320 rpm. It had such a distinctive sound, a slow Tabang-Tabang-Tabang. The Scania is faster but now we use 60 litres of fuel an hour instead of only 9! Many of these Luxemotors were lengthened and deepened to carry more load, when this was done the flowing lines vanished, I could not do that to my ship, she is just too beautiful". His father also has a large motor-ship and for many years they worked in tandem.

The second section of the luxemotor is the engine-room. The engine-room could at last be designed around the motor, rather than the other way round. Engines of this era were massively built and an engine with large amounts of horsepower took up large amounts of space. A typical twin-cylinder diesel of 80 hp, for example the van Berkel of 1923, would stand three metres tall, with a huge solid outside flywheel of around two or three tons. This, coupled with the ancillary air-compressor for starting, plus fuel and oil tanks, not to mention the gearbox and drive shaft, took up a lot of space. There was no compromise however and most luxemotors that I have visited have airy, well lit, engine-rooms, with plenty of working space, even those still retaining their old massive motors. A metal bulkhead with a watertight and flameproof door separates the cargo space from the engine space. The tall motors of the time meant that a small raised roef as seen on the earlier beurtmotors was needed. This gave space for the motor, whilst a series of portholes around the sides allowed ventilation and a little light. On top of this short motorroef (which is a distinctive feature originally unique to the luxemotor and beurtmotor types) is the wheel-house. The lower section was, in most cases, constructed from steel, with the upper section built of wood. The top section may be dismantled for passing under bridges. The wheel-house has a door on both port and starboard, although the port-side is generally provided with a platform, a step and hand-rails.

Directly behind the port-side access steps is the engine-room hatch, with a steel ladder giving access. These ladders are steep, mostly covered in a thin film of diesel oil and immensely slippery when wet. It is normal practice to keep the engine-room hatch open whilst under way, as this helps to allow the engine to breath. Inevitably, at some time water will get on to these steps. Familiarity breeds contempt, or at least complacency and a prudent skipper or engineer will always descend these steps backwards, with one hand for the ship at all times. Many people I have spoken to have fallen down these steps. Whilst working on the luxemotor "Vertrouwen" in Scotland, I fell victim to complacency and cracked two ribs. I was forced to carry on working in extreme pain until they healed. I hope that I for one have learnt my lesson.

As mentioned earlier, the wheel-house may be dismantled. In theory this is fairly simple, but in practice, as the comfortable warm cabin becomes part of the living space, it becomes full of papers, pot plants and coffee cups. For the metre or so saved, it is often just as well to wait for the bridge to open, or pick another route. At the rear of the wheel-house, on the port side, is the access to the third section, the living space or salonroef. Traditionally this is light and airy, totally unlike the cramped achteronder of the previous century. Because of the shape of the counter-stern and the location of the propeller shaft, the roef is built well above deck level to allow full standing headroom. This means that good-sized windows can be incorporated. Here is to be found a toilet and washroom, a small kitchen, a dining-sitting room and a good-sized bedroom. When finances allowed it, the shipyard carpenter could really express himself here. Working in conjunction with the owner and his wife, he could incorporate cupboards, etched glass panelled doors and different shades and grains of wood into the fit-out. Tropical hardwoods were popular and where more humble panelling was to be employed, the use of "gehout" was common. Gehout (in England called scumbling), is simply the practice of using stains and paint to apply a uniform artificial grain to the surface. For the skipper's wife in particular this was indeed a luxury motor-ship. The name luxemotor was born and it was soon universally applied to any ship built along these lines.

48) Luxemotor *"Flora"*, one of the first pleasure boats on the Rijn.

49) *"Cornelia"* forging her way upstream between towed dumb barges.

On the deck, to the rear of the salonroef, is a small after-deck which allows access to the rudder hangings and steering quadrant. A stern anchor with dedicated hawse-hole is also fitted. Whilst all luxemotors have a counter-stern, as mentioned earlier those built in the north differ to those built in the west. The western built ships have an almost 90 degree angle between the counter and the boeisel. This is called a "motorhek". The northern built ships have, in general, a much blunter shape, with a correspondingly less severe angle between counter and boeisel. In these cases the ship is said to have a "kruiserhek". In extreme cases the stern above the counter is almost vertical. In both models the counter ends at the normal loaded waterline and below this is the propeller aperture.

Unlike the spits, the luxemotor did not have to comply with any specific dimensional criteria. From the beginning of their building-life, they tended towards economical practical size, rather than maximum allowable size. Typically, a luxemotor of the 1920's was 25m in length by 5m in the beam. This allowed free navigation on the majority of the waterways of the Netherlands. By the crisis years of the depression in 1929-30, which saw an enormous over-capacity of shipping tonnage and many hungry skippers, the luxemotor continued to flourish and grew in length to a typical 30m, whilst still retaining a 5m beam. The crisis years aside, 1920 to 1940 were the glory years for the luxemotor. In 1930, some enterprising skippers seeking to widen their field of trade, were running tourist ships up and down the Rijn, predating the current hotel-barge scene by thirty or forty years. The second world war saw virtually all the larger ships taken by the invading Germans for war work. Some found their way to the Russian lakes and others to the Mediterranean. A vast number of luxemotors, spitsen and klippers alike, were simply converted to troop landing craft ready for Operation Sealion, the planned invasion of England. In the end, with air supremacy never established over the channel and a new front opening up in the east, the invasion never took place. After the war most of the requisitioned ships were reclaimed by their owners and reconverted back to cargo carriers (see chapter nine).

After the war, although many were lengthened and deepened to allow them to remain in trade, no more true luxemotors were built. By 1950 it was becoming more and more difficult for relatively small ships to compete for trade with the newer, larger ships. However, if you keep your eyes open when travelling in the Netherlands, you will still find original luxemotors (some even miraculously un-lengthened) in service commercially.

50) The 250 ton luxemotor *"International"* has been lengthened and deepened to the "Freycinet" size of 38 by 8.5m.

51) Luxemotor *"Volharding 2"* loading sacks of grain in the Coolhaven in Rotterdam. The skipper and mate handle the sacks whilst the skipper's wife manages the winch.

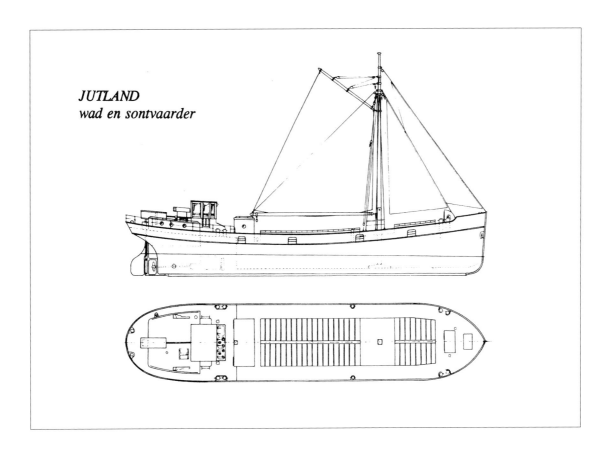

JUTLAND
wad en sontvaarder

52/53) Wad & Sontvaarders.

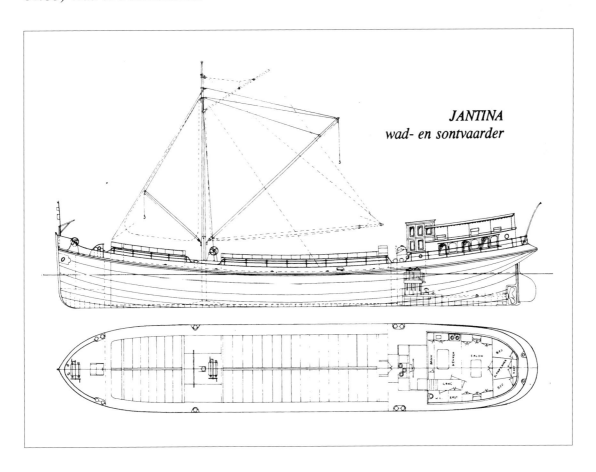

JANTINA
wad- en sontvaarder

Wad, Belt & Sontvaarders

A special type of luxemotor was built to trade on the coastal routes and also to venture onto the Baltic. They acquired the name of their sailing ancestors, which at that time were still a major force in the northern trade. These ships sailed along the Waddenzee coast, through what was the Keizer Willem Kanaal, now the Noord-Oostzeekanaal (or Kiel Kanaal) to trade in Sweden and Denmark. The Sont is the area of water that lies between the Swedish coast and the island of Sjaelland. The Belt, comprising the Grote Belt, Kleine Belt and Fehrman Belt, is in Danish water around the island of Fyn.

Built mainly after 1930, these are more massively built ships, with a full length keelson, deeper draft and generally coaster-like appearance, whilst still retaining the luxemotor features. The Beltvaarder was the closest to the luxemotor in appearance, whilst the Wad and Sont ships have more seagoing features, such as smaller wheel-houses, wider side-decks, smaller hatches, and portholes rather than windows in the roef. These were all 30m or more in length, with a wider beam of up to 6.5m. Some had a truly useful sailing-rig, but most retained a mast purely for loading.

One typical example of a Sontvaarder is *"Jantina"*, built in Groningen in 1926, measuring 31 by 5.32m and drawing 2.2m fully loaded. *"Jantina"* originally had a two-cylinder Kromhout engine of 60 hp. Requisitioned by the Germans during the war and subsequently sunk in a British air raid, she survives today with a larger 140 hp twin Kromhout.

As was the case with nearly all the successful binnenvaart and kustvaart ships, most Wad and Sontvaarders were lengthened and deepened to keep pace with the demands of trade. However, if a small enough example can still be found for sale, there is no doubting their able-ness. The *"Adriana"*, loading 145 tons and built to "Friese maat" (Friese dimensions) of 31.5 by 5.4m, was built in Hoogezand at the "Coop" shipyard in 1925. She was taken over by the invading Germans in 1942 and an intriguing surviving report shows that on the 9th of October 1943, the *"Adriana"* was taking part in an anti-partisan operation, against Yugoslavian guerrillas, in the Adriatic sea. Sadly that is the last report, but maybe she is still tucked away somewhere, or even still working in some guise or another. It is certainly possible.

English coasting barges

As mentioned in the chapter on motors, at the same time as motorizing was occurring in Holland, a similar process was occurring in England. In fact it is true to say that there was a certain amount of cross-over regarding engineering ideas. Some skippers bought coasting barges from Holland and Kromhout engines were often seen in otherwise all-English coasters. A very few barges were built in England for use on the continent. In Holland these gained the derogatory name of "Engelseebakken" (English buckets), reflecting the basic, functional build, devoid of flair or good looks. In England the circumstances in which most barges were employed were somewhat different to those occurring in Holland and here evolution took a slightly different route. However, in the area of the smaller coasting barges there are some striking similarities. Certainly if you are lucky enough to come across a preserved example and you have limited offshore objectives, then it is worth as much consideration as its Dutch counterpart. As with the Dutch ships, engines first appeared as auxiliary units, but by 1920, the same year as the luxemotor appeared, English barges were being built in which it was the sails not the engine that was the auxiliary factor. In 1920 the Wynfield Shipping Co. of Grimsby commissioned the 375 ton "Wessex". She was 30.9m in length and 6.8m in the beam.

The *"Wessex"* is similar to the Dutch ship *"Jantina"*, mentioned earlier, with dimensions of 31.03 by 5.32m. The *"Wessex"* predates *"Jantina"* by some five years, but both ships are typical of the small coasters of the time. The English ships were still being built of wood in some cases and in a wood-steel composite in others. Composite ships would have primarily wooden planking and decks, but built over a framework of steel frames, knees and stringers.

One rather English convention that was very rarely adopted by the Dutch, was that of installing twin screw propulsion units. Many of the engines used in English barges were still coming from the Netherlands, but these were large and bulky for only a modest horsepower. By installing two identical engines side by side, space was saved, and arguably by using two small screws instead of one large one, it was possible to keep the propeller immersed even when travelling light. An insufficiently immersed propeller is a problem that even today many motor-barges and sailing-barge conversions suffer from. For instance, the *"Rochester Castle"* was designed and built by Short Brothers of Rochester in 1923, fitted with twin screws, a wooden hull and lines reminiscent of a luxemotor. She has a straight, pointed stem, a little sheer and a counter-stern. On deck the wheel-house is set forward of what is undeniably a variation of the classic Dutch salonroef. The short mast is set right forward and able to set a modest amount of sail for work off the wind. In so many ways she seems to embrace more ideas from across the channel than those from nearer to home.

Another ship of similar vintage was the *"Heather Pet"*, built in Sittingbourne, Kent, by Wills and Packham. She too had a length of 30m and loaded 250 tons for coastal work. She was of the semi-composite type of construction, with a wooden, hard chine hull over steel frames. Once again she had a straight stem and counter-stern. Deep in her engine-room was an English engine that showed the shape of things to come. Whilst other ships were still using the reliable, but technically old fashioned Kromhout type motors, *"Heather Pet"* had a 110 hp Vickers Petter engine, with a reverse gear, direct fuel injection and electric starting.

Quaintly, where both the *"Heather Pet"* and the *"Rochester Castle"* differ considerably from their Dutch equivalents, is in the provision of a smoke-stack type chimney, reminiscent of a steam-boat, rather than the simple exhaust favoured by their continental colleagues, but then, English coastal routes were not often bothered by low bridges!

CHAPTER NINE

Operation Sealion

In June 1940, the Germans had occupied most of western Europe, with the notable exception of the British Isles. There has always been much debate about Hitler's commitment to an invasion of England. Whatever the circumstances, the planning of Operation Sealion, the invasion of southern England from the sea, was instigated and much time and effort went into it throughout the summer and autumn of 1940.

Where does this all fit into a book about motor-barges? To cross an expanse of water an army needs boats, lots of them. The coastal and inland shipping fleet of western Europe had plenty of these, in all shapes and sizes.

Initial plans suggested, that given sufficient numbers of un-motorized barges, the necessary powered barges, tugs, fishing boats etc, could be quite quickly found to pull the troop and supply carrying barges across the channel. Criteria concerning seaworthiness and strength were drawn up and four major points relating to the possible use of what were essentially inland trading barges arose.

1)........ The barges must be able to cope safely with a full load in sea states of up to state two (exercises were in fact carried out in winds up to force six with no appreciable problems and only minor damage).

2)........ They must be able to ground safely on a beach with a gradient of one degree and be able to re-float.

3)....... They must have the structural strength to carry a minimum of one 25 ton tank along with troops and equipment.

4) .... They must be of a size that enabled them to use the canals and waterways of the Netherlands, Belgium and northern France.

From these criteria it became clear that an internal depth of hold of 2m was necessary. A basic formula suggested that ships with a length to depth (of hold) ratio of 12-15/1 would be suitable. Many of the inland barges had a ratio of 25 or even 35/1. A compromise figure of 19/1 was finally agreed on and in the case of particularly strongly built ships this could be increased to 22/1. It is these facts that resulted in many potentially seaworthy barges of the tjalk and klipper types, along with the smaller motor-barges, being rejected. In some small way this contributed to the fact that today there are so many of these smaller ships still surviving. The barges that did comply with these criteria were mainly the peniche and spits types (at that time almost universally without motors), the luxemotors, Kempenaars, kasten and the larger klippers. Searches of the records of the inland shipping registration records showed, that at first glance 860 ships were available from German sources, mainly Rhine ships, 1200 from the Netherlands and Belgium and 350 from France. Of these 2410 ships, approximately 800 were shown as being motorized, but German sources show that of these 800, barely 30% were rated as sufficiently powerful to be truly self-propelled. The others being basically low powered auxiliary units.

Memo to the German Naval High Command from the Merchant Shipping Division, June 13th 1940 : "although 2000 barges are available, many of the Rhine vessels are not considered as being suitable for the purpose of carrying troops and equipment due to their lack of sea-worthiness and low longitudinal strength".

A conference was held on the 26th July to iron out foreseeable problems and to get the initial stages of Sealion underway. It was made very clear, that to prepare 2000 barges and associated support ships in the time stipulated (one month), would cause severe problems in all areas of wartime commerce. Simply moving all the barges to the conversion yards would tie up virtually all the available inland cargo fleet, with severe implications for defence, food and transport. Over 30,000 tons of steel would be needed, 40,000 cubic metres of timber and 75,000 cubic metres of cement. In addition, all the shipyards on the Rhine and the Dutch estuary would need to be exclusively given over to the project for four weeks (in the event virtually all the major shipyards in the western Netherlands, including such famous names as "van de Giezen" at Krimpen a/d IJssel, became involved, along with most of those in Belgium and northern France).

The orders went out to commandeer the relevant barges and to assemble them at the shipyards which would make the necessary modifications.

As this all progressed, it was noted that many of the available barges seemed very hard to find and were often finally located in small side canals and tributaries in remote locations. This is not really surprising, as the owners and skippers of these ships could still make some kind of living during war time and in many instances the requisition order meant not just the loss of income, but also the loss of the only home that the skipper and his family had. In addition, it became apparent that a great number of barges were arriving at the shipyards with serious defects. How much of this was down to fate and how much the people of the occupied countries helped fate along, can only be guessed at.

The requisitioned barges all fell into two basic categories. Types A1 and A2.

Type A1 was basically any barge up to the basic spits/peniche size of 38.5 by 5.05m.

Type A2 was simply any barge not in the first category. These were mainly of the Kempenaar type, generally 50 by 5.5m.

Conversion work on the barges was carried out in Germany as well as the occupied countries. Unsurprisingly, work in the German yards appeared to be quicker and more efficient than that carried out elsewhere. Eventually, military construction battalions were drafted in to aid the civilian workers where appropriate.

The first stage of modification, for all the barges, was to strengthen them longitudinally for the sea crossing. Diagonal braces were welded into the sides at about every sixth frame and attached to the frames and deck beams by knees. The floor of the hold needed to be strong enough to take the weight of several tanks and so three "I" section rails were welded into place, attached to the bottom frames on each side of the hold, to form a track-way for the tank's treads. All the bays between the frames were filled with concrete. A spits/peniche could take three tanks and the larger Kempenaar four. The smaller type A1 barges could carry one tank and a mixture of trucks, horses, bicycles, artillery etc.

54) A barge with cut away bow, but no internal strengthening yet installed.

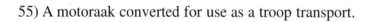

55) A motoraak converted for use as a troop transport.

Without doubt, the most obvious modification was to the bows of the ships of type A1. The bow was completely cut away, "gekopt" (beheaded), and a landing ramp installed forward of a watertight bulkhead. This bulkhead had to be well above the loaded waterline and so an additional ramp was built into the barge, to allow vehicles to drive up and over the bulkhead and then down the ramp onto the beach. This modification made little difference to an already blunt bowed spits, but for a river ship with a pointed stem, or a beautiful klipper bow, a large section had to be removed to gain the necessary width to allow vehicles to disembark. Other modifications included the fitting of bow and stern anchors (if not already installed), life-rafts, bicycle-racks and horse-stalls (at this time "modern" warfare was still in the early stages of becoming truly mechanized and the long suffering horse served to provide much of the "horsepower" for the German army in all areas of conflict, from the south of France to Stalingrad). In some cases defensive armament was fitted, usually on a gun platform amidships, this varied from anti-tank to anti-aircraft guns, along with a pedestal mounted machine-gun. It is also interesting to note that many of the barges were fitted with rudder blades that were far too big for use in anything except still water. In these cases they were modified to a size more in keeping with a sea going motor-ship. Finally, all the iron and steel barges were degaussed to give them some protection from magnetic mines.

The largest of the type A2 barges, designated A2(C), carried the wider amphibious tanks fitted with floats (Panzer II, *"schwimmpanzer"*), these had no need to actually run themselves aground and so they were modified by cutting away the stern to allow the tanks to exit to the rear whilst the barge was still well afloat. This all meant that the wheel-house and accommodation were removed and a smaller raised steering position was built onto the starboard side above the lowering ramp. In this way, up to four tanks at a time could be loaded from a larger ship in deep water and disembarked close to the shore.

For all the barges designed to disembark directly onto the beach there was one very major problem; they could only be used on a gently shelving beach on a falling tide. This meant that not only would the invading troops have a wide expanse of beach to cross before finding cover, but the barges would have to sit on the beach at the low water mark until the tide re-floated them. The reason being that there were simply not enough barges to allow them to be run ashore and abandoned. They had to be able to make several return trips to their mother ships in deep water, or even back across the channel to the Schelde, a one-way trip of around 15 hours.

Other specifically designated barge types were the type B, AS and AF.

The type B was modified in the same fashion as a type A1 or A2, but was not intended to run aground, instead it would anchor in around 4m of water and disembark one or more semi-submersible tanks fitted with a snorkel breathing device. When unloaded they could return to the mother ship for another consignment, without having to wait for a tide to re-float them.

Type AS was a troop carrying barge designed to bring the first wave of assault troops ashore. It did not have to carry heavy armour, just troops and light assault boats. Again, as with the type B, these had no need to go aground and would keep making return trips to deeper water. They were modified to give greater protection to the troops by lining the sides of the hold with reinforced concrete.

Type AF is particularly relevant to a book concerning motor-barges. Somehow the German air-force (Luftwaffe) had got involved. At this stage of the war they had several hundred BMW 6U aircraft engines that had exceeded their allotted number of air hours. The Luftwaffe engineers decided to have a go at barge motorization.

The aero-engines were 12 cylinder, water cooled engines, developing 600 hp. It was found that by mounting two engines, complete with propellers, side by side on the aft end of the barges, mostly spits/peniche and Kempenaars, a reasonable speed of 6 knots could be developed, even towing one or more barges alongside and astern. Although theoretically the range of a barge so fitted was around 60 kilometres, it was not deemed practical to cross the channel in this way. They would be towed across by tugs or fishing boats, in the same way as all the other barges, until close to the shore. The plan then was to link up to six un-powered barges behind one of the aero-engined barges. The aero-engines would be started up about two or three kilometres from the landing site, allowing them to build up to full speed before arriving on the beach, the powered vessel would drive itself ashore and the others, propelled by inertia, would follow suit. The thought of a spits, or Kempenaar, hurtling towards the shore with a couple of thousand horsepower on its stern, hotly pursued by half a dozen other barges is a truly scary vision. It is hard to work out who would have been the most scared, the defending troops on the beaches, or the soldiers of the Wehrmacht cowering inside the "flying boats!"

The crewing arrangements for the barges were as diverse as the barges themselves. The navy (Kriegsmarine) supplied some key personnel, but did not have enough spare, trained seamen and so they had to be sought elsewhere. The barges requisitioned from German sources were to keep their original civilian skippers and crew and it was planned to man all the other non-German barges with other German civilian personnel. All the harbour and river authorities were scoured for suitable men, eventually this extended to deeming pre-war membership of a yacht or sailing club to be suitable experience. At one stage it was found that teenage boys were being recruited from school sailing clubs and drafted into operation Sealion. This was too much even for the German Naval Office, which on learning of this, immediately de-mobilized them and sent them back to school (it is sad to think that just four years later boys of the same age would be fighting and dying in defence of their country). Training was very basic. All crews, serving naval ranks, professional seamen and civilians alike, attended a two day training course at Emden, followed by a ten day course at Rotterdam. Conscripted personnel also had the dubious benefit of five weeks military basic training. Crews on the un-powered barges comprised a skipper and three crewmen, powered craft also had an engineer, whilst the type AF barges, fitted with aero-engines, carried two Luftwaffe flight mechanics.

Finding and training all these men in a country already at war was no easy task, but in the end, just under 12000 men were trained and ready to crew the invasion barges.

OTHER SEALION VESSELS.

Of course the invasion barges were useless on their own, many other ships were needed to enable the operation to succeed. Motor-boats were needed to push and pull the barges and larger ships to carry the necessary equipment and supplies to back up the invading troops. Coasters and small cargo ships were commandeered from the occupied countries, as well as from Germany itself. At one stage it was thought that the practice of using a small pusher boat, or "opduwer", as was widely used in the Netherlands, might be a possibility, but it was found that using this method at sea was slow and unreliable. In this way the Netherlands fleet of opduwers was saved. Tugs were a more practical proposition and there were enough of these in the Netherlands alone. Unfortunately the vast majority of these ships were steam tugs and worse still, relied on fresh river-water to allow their condensing systems to work. They were no use in salt water. The Dutch steam-boat fleet was also saved.

In the end, supplies of harbour tugs were brought from mainly German sources. The Netherlands did however have a large fleet of small motor-coasters and auxiliary sailing vessels, as well as a great many motor-fishing-boats. Wad- and Sont-vaarders, schoeners, zee-klippers, Lemsteraken and kotters, all were commandeered into the Sealion fleet. The fishing-boats were to be used as tugs, to pull the barges across the channel and then to retrieve them from the beaches to be re-loaded offshore. The larger coasters, 100-200 tons, would be used as supply ships. The smaller coasting vessels, the schoeners and klippers with their shallow draft, could get close inshore to launch assault boats and troops. In some ways the klippers treated this way got off lightly in the conversion yards. They were mostly fitted with a gun platform for mounting 37-105 mm guns, but, it was stated;

"these mounts may be constructed of wood, as it is not anticipated that any return voyages will be necessary".

Because the coasters would not be run ashore like the assault barges, there was no need to cut their bows away to form ramps. Most of the schoeners and klippers were fitted with a removable, aft-facing, ramp. This was to be slotted into position, prior to landing, just forward of the lee-board position. The assault boats and troops were carried in the hold and on deck, with the vessels cargo derrick being used to place the assault boats on the ramps. These would then be launched by simply sliding down the ramps. The ramps were made of plywood on wooden frames, as were the assault boats themselves. These small craft carried six troops and a helmsman and were fitted with a 30 hp Otto outboard motor.

River and harbour ferries could also be used, as they were already designed to carry road vehicles. Many of these self-propelled ferries, both steam and diesel powered, were conscripted into the fleet. Railway ferries were also used and the ferry *"Moerdijk"*, which was kept in German service after Sealion was abandoned, eventually saw service in September 1944, when the retreating German army used it to withdraw across the Schelde.

For all these other vessels crews had to be found and trained. In addition to those found for the barges, an extra 2768 helmsmen, 913 engineers, 1159 steam engine mechanics, 2027 boiler-men and 449 tug skippers were eventually made ready for duty.

I won't go into the many reasons that Sealion did not take place, in any case the true facts are still being argued over by military historians. However, as we know, it never happened and when it was eventually called off, most of the requisitioned and converted barges were kept for general war work. Many of the German owned ships were returned to their owners and some of the coasting vessels and tugs. The bulk of the Dutch, Belgian and French ships however were retained. Some went on to see service in the waters off Norway, the Baltic, Mediterranean, Aegean and the Black Sea; some even found their way to the Russian lakes.

Of course, whilst all this was going on, the tjalken, aken, steilstevens and bols were quietly continuing to go about their business. Ideally suited to manage without fossil fuels to keep them going, too small or un-seaworthy for war service and with crews considered (rightly so) unlikely to be conscientious and reliable workers for German masters, they continued to sail and pull their ships along the canals as they had for the last fifty years or more.

56) The Belgian Spits *"Fingle of Caledonia"* (ex *"Timor"*), now works in Scotland alongside the luxemotors *"Vertrouwen"* and *"Spirit of Loch Ness"* (ex *"Corry III"*).

57) The different bow shapes of *"Vertrouwen"* and *"Corry III"* respectively, are those of a river ship and a canal ship. The sharp bow cuts through the water easier, but the blunt shape can load more cargo.

CHAPTER TEN

Cruising with a luxemotor

"The art of handling a ship is finer perhaps, than the art of handling men"
Joseph Conrad

I had cause to remember these words in 1996, when I was employed as the skipper of the hotel barge *"Vertrouwen"*, travelling the Caledonian canal in the highlands of Scotland. During that time we travelled around 2000 miles together and some of my impressions and experiences are detailed here (those of ship handling anyway, my experiences of man management are entirely the subject for another book)! Whilst these experiences cannot be said to hold true for all luxemotors, they are typical of the breed. I have met with Meneer Jaap Oosterlee, the previous commercial skipper of the ship and after talking at great length, have found that many of our experiences are common to both commercial and pleasure trading.

"Vertrouwen" is a luxemotor, with the sharp bow of a river ship. She was built in Vreeswijk in 1931 and fitted from new with a twin-cylinder Brons diesel engine. After the second world war she was lengthened to her present size of 36m. In 1961 a British built Gardner 6LX replaced the Brons. Originally registered in Utrecht, from the mid sixties up to 1989 she carried sand and gravel in the Rotterdam area under skipper Jaap Oosterlee, from Maassluis. After a major facelift in 1990 she moved north to Scotland and began work on the Caledonian canal.

Externally, apart from the hatch-boards being replaced with a one-piece steel deck, *"Vertrouwen"* remains essentially the same as when she carried sand and gravel. Down below of course things have changed considerably, but when underway she behaves in the same manner as when skipper Jaap Oosterlee made his return trips to Rotterdam. With an anti-clockwise propeller when in forward, *"Vertrouwen's"* stern tends to pull to port when getting away. This can mean that she will try to drag her port quarter along the side of the quay or lock. To remedy this, it is necessary to first apply a little port helm and then by giving the engine a light kick ahead, the stern swings out as the bow swings in. If the helm is then straightened up, the paddle-wheel effect from the propeller brings the stern and bow back into line, now safely away from the quay-side. Even though she is in effect travelling "light", *"Vertrouwen"* nevertheless possesses tremendous inertia when in motion and this must be taken into consideration when docking or entering a lock.

Going astern is a different matter entirely. At the northern end of the Caledonian canal, in Inverness, the canal runs down a flight of five locks into a basin. Here *"Vertrouwen"* could be turned around in readiness for the return journey south to Fort William. This all took time, about three hours to negotiate both ways. A quarter of a mile above the top lock is a winding hole, of just sufficient width to allow *"Vertrouwen"* to complete a 180°turn. The problem then was to reverse the ship a quarter of a mile back into our berth by the top lock. I developed a technique that worked and as the year wore on took a delight in the manoeuvre.

The trick was to enter the winding hole slowly, as far to port as possible and as soon as the stern had passed the pontoons of Cally Marina, a hard turn to starboard was initiated, sometimes I would get it just right and we would turn in our own length, at other times it was necessary to push the bow gently into the bank and use this as a fulcrum to complete the turn. Having achieved a successful reversal it was time to go astern for the last quarter mile of the journey. *"Vertrouwen"* would never go astern in a straight line. The shape of the hull, the rotation of the propeller and the depth of immersion, all conspire to thwart the skipper. The only way was to go astern at about half revs, the ship would then go backwards and slowly turn in an anti-clockwise direction. When this turn became too acute a burst of full ahead was given, with the helm hard over to starboard. This would straighten the ship and whilst she was still straightening up, astern was applied once more. In this way the ship built up momentum in the required direction and would continue to go astern even whilst forward power was straightening up the inherent swing. When this whole manoeuvre went smoothly (it didn't always) it was immensely satisfying and never failed to raise a round of applause from the paying guests.

I only once had the opportunity to asses *"Vertrouwen's"* characteristics in rough water. It was on Loch Ness, at the start of the season and a gale had been blowing for two days. This built up a fairly big sea moving from south to north. I contacted the owner of the ship who had skippered her for the previous two years and consequently knew her better than I did. He said that a force 8 gale was no problem on the nose. After one day waiting for the wind to decrease, we ducked out of our berth in Foyers and turned around the point heading south for Fort Augustus. As we emerged from the lee of the point, the ensuing rolling motion was extreme to say the least.

Happily, of course, this soon decreased as we turned into the wind and sea. Heading dead into the waves, we made good progress amidst much spray. Occasionally an extra big wave would induce a shudder that could be felt all over the ship and on one occasion we fell off one of these large waves into a deep trough.

That was the only time I was at all worried. There was a shuddering crash, the bow disappeared from sight, spray covered the wheel-house windows and when vision was restored I was relieved to see that the ship was still in one piece. After that, as we neared Fort Augustus, the sea decreased and the guests appeared on deck once more.

58) *"Vertrouwen"* on Loch Lochy, a section of the Caledonian Canal, in the Highlands of Scotland.

CHAPTER ELEVEN
Cargo management

In most of today's barge conversions, the wooden hatch-boards and loading derrick are removed to fit a purpose-built deckhouse. However, some still cruise quite successfully whilst retaining many original features. The items that I propose to describe are typical of a Dutch built ship, but are in essence true for all the ships described in this book.

Hulptuig

This is the sailing-rig fitted to many of the first motor-ships. It is simply a scaled down version of that found on the true sailing-barges, but designed to help the ship's progress, not provide the sole motive power. A ship fitted with a hulptuig as original equipment, invariably had a "mastdek" (see "hijstuig", below) two-thirds of the way along the ship's length, with additional cargo space in front of it. A small, conventional loose footed cotton mainsail on a small gaff was flown behind the mast and a small jib, often on its own boom, forward of this. Raising the sails and manipulating the boom for cargo handling was carried out in the same way as for the hijstuig (see below). Since the rig was un-ambitious and lee-boards were, in most cases, no longer carried, the hulptuig was only really any use down-wind. However, when used in conjunction with the main engine, it saved some fuel and gave a little extra speed. In truth many of the skippers had been raised on sailing-barges and although a luxury motor-ship was attractive, the motor was still treated with a little suspicion. The hulptuig gave the skipper confidence that he could get out of trouble in case of engine failure. For pleasure use, I think that a motor-ship with traditional hulptuig looks lovely. The hassle involved in lowering the mast is nothing compared to the ability to shut down the motor occasionally and drift along in silence. It seems to me a shame, that so many converted ships have only a stumpy little mast, of no use for anything but carrying the wind flags.

Hijstuig

This is a mast and boom arrangement used exclusively for cargo management. It may be of wood, or more likely steel construction. The mast itself is deck-stepped on a strengthened area of the ship, called the "mastdek". The base of the whole rig is the "mastkoker" (tabernacle), which forms the steel support for the mast and also incorporates the framework for the winches. The mast pivots on a lateral pin, which passes through both the mast and the mastkoker. It is prevented from falling forwards by the closed rear of the mastkoker, whilst the open front allows it to be lowered towards the rear of the ship. Another pin, usually with a wooden wedge, located in front of the mast at its foot, secures the mast in an upright position. Its removal allows the mast to be lowered under control. Depending on the height and weight of the mast, between one and three shrouds may be used. In this fashion it is possible to lower the mast when necessary with minimum fuss. At the masthead are the necessary blocks to allow articulation of the boom. This part of the rig is secured to the after side of the mastkoker by a gooseneck comprising two pins: one vertical with an eye at the top, free to rotate in a fitting called the "lummelpot" and the other passing through the boom and the eye in the first pin. This arrangement allows free movement of the boom in all planes.

Hijstuigen

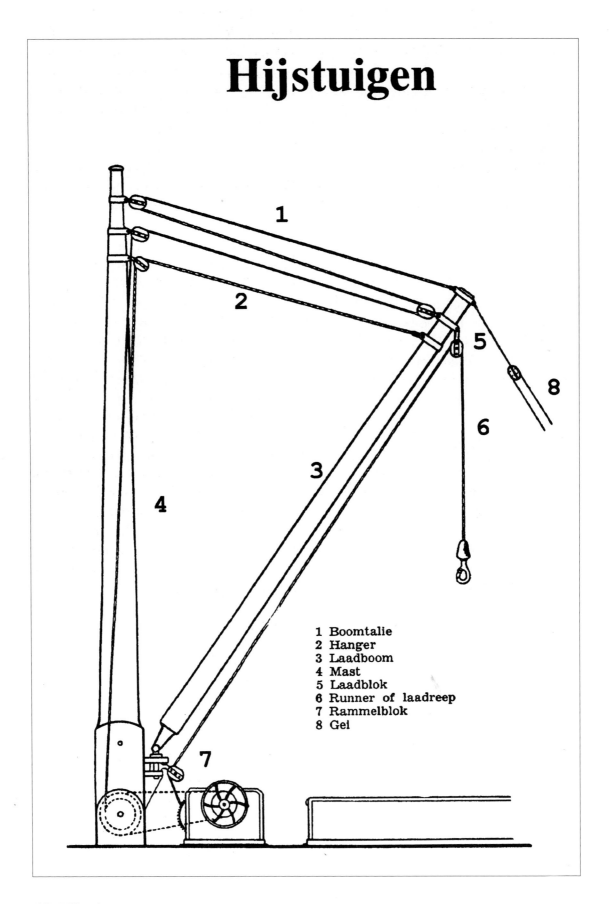

1 Boomtalie
2 Hanger
3 Laadboom
4 Mast
5 Laadblok
6 Runner of laadreep
7 Rammelblok
8 Gei

59) Hijstuigen

At the base of the mastkoker are the winches which manipulate the boom, raise and lower the cargo hooks and also serve to lower the mast. These are generally very robust pieces of machinery and to me very attractive, especially if they retain the lovely hand-wheels with the curved spokes. On larger ships a separate deck mounted engine, in conjunction with a simple friction clutch, will be used. Some may have an engine below deck driving the hijstuig winches and also the anchor winch, whilst others have a generator room powering the winches by belts and often converting to three phase 220v A/C electrical power.

The really large ships, with substantial cargo space forward of the mast, will probably have a second, forward facing boom, to handle cargo in the forward areas. Truly modern ships may have an hydraulically operated crane to lift a car or two on board.

Ankerlier

Most of the smaller ex-sailing-ships were never fitted with an anchor winch, as the weight of the anchors was low and the necessity to use them was rare. Larger ships were forced to use winches and on the early ships this was a wooden barrel with the chain wrapped around it several times. This would be turned by means of a spike being inserted into slots in the barrel, or by means of a belt or chain from the winches beneath the mast. Mechanical winches did not become really common until around 1910. However, before this, even many of the large ships managed all by block and tackle. As winches became available they were gratefully received, not least to take the effort out of mast lowering, a common occurrence on the sailing river-ships. Today it is most likely that a winch or two will be fitted. Even if the mast no longer serves any purpose other than to fly flags, it is almost certain that at least an anchor winch will remain. On small ships this will be a simple hand-operated affair, whilst most of the larger ships have a more sophisticated set-up. On luxemotors and other motor-ships, this will probably consist of a double set of gearwheels, each driving its own gypsy, for each of the two bow anchors carried. In addition, warping drums may be incorporated. The winch can be used manually (I've done it myself), but due to the very low gearing it is not practical except in an emergency. In almost all cases the winch will be driven by mechanical, electrical, or hydraulic means from the ship's generator.

Luiken

The hold of a cargo ship, whether engaged in inland or coastal trade, needs to be totally watertight, yet also have the capability of being fully opened quickly and easily for loading. When mechanical grabs, cranes, suction pumps and hoppers became commonplace, a completely uncluttered hold was essential for efficient and easy working. Apart from the smallest of ships, all the inland ships at the turn of the century had a single longitudinal wooden beam, the "scheerboom" or "scheerbalk". This formed the spine for the hatches and was higher than the coamings to allow a water repellent camber to be formed. On the top of the scheerboom was the "kapdeksel" (a flat capping strip), which made the whole beam into a "T" shape. Athwartship beams, called "merkels", were positioned every metre or so, depending on the width and strength of the "luiken". In the case of a ship with a wooden scheerboom the merkels were ftted into slots in the scheerboom, under the kapdeksel. The outboard end was laid into a notch in the den. The merkel had a small recess cut along its length in the centre which married up to a corresponding strip laying proud on the end of the luiken.

The outboard end of the luiken had a hasp on them that fitted over an eye in the den and was then secured with a long pin, rope, or wire. Since all the parts were individually and uniquely constructed, every beam and every luik had to be individually numbered to ensure a good reliable fit.

On top of the luiken, tarred clothes would be laid, lashed down to form a watertight, weatherproof, covering. A seagoing ship would be similarly equipped, but might have three scheerbomen and use double layers of tarred cloth lashed in place, then finally secured by chains and tackles. Although the authorities set a lower limit on the quantity of cargo carried in exposed waters, thus ensuring a higher freeboard, it was still vitally important to maintain watertight integrity when venturing offshore. The introduction of lightweight, waterproof, aluminium luiken in later years, made trading safer and loading quicker.

60) The 175 ton *"Hestor"*. The scheerboom and merkels are clearly visible along with the individually numbered, tarred wooden hatches, made from three planks. The join is sealed with tarred rope.

61) The hatches on *"Internationaal"* are original, but in this case the den has been almost doubled in height. The hasp and eye fastening is clearly visible.

To the original skippers, the hold was probably the part of the ship that was most important to them. This was the area that earned them their living. In many cases they spent as much time working in the hold as they did sailing the ship; certainly more time was spent here than in the roef. A working day of twelve hours or more was normal practice. Remaining ships that still have the original wooden hatch-boards in place are not uncommon. It is, therefore, well worthwhile knowing the names of the component parts and their importance to the watertight integrity and structural soundness of the hull. Many of these parts may be referred to in ship's documentation and knowing their name and purpose may be of interest (some you will have already encountered in previous sections). The sides of the hold (coaming) above the side decks are referred to as the "den". Metal deck-beams known as "gebinten", running athwartship, are positioned at intervals along the length of the den. They may be straight, curved, or double curved. They serve to help keep the sides of the ship stable, neither being pushed outwards by the cargo or pushed inwards by external water pressure. They are removable to allow easy loading. In small ships with a low hold space, repeated concussion from cranial collisions with gebinten may tempt the owner to remove them to allow more headroom. If the hatch-boards are not replaced with a substantial steel coach-roof at the same time, which itself must be supported by athwartship strengtheners, this may seriously weaken the ship, rendering it potentially dangerous at sea. The hatch-boards themselves are made from individual lengths of plank. These may number four or five in flat boards, or be more numerous in the curving Friese luiken. The planks are slotted together and the join is either covered by a length of jute soaked in brown-tar, pinned in position with copper tacks, or a bead of wood may be pressed into the brown-tar filled joint. The boards themselves would originally be regularly soaked in boiled linseed oil. When the luiken were all in place, along with the merkels, and fastened securely in place by hasp and eye, the whole area was covered with coal-tarred cloth. This was lashed in place and for a sea crossing it might in addition have extra beams, double clothes and chains to hold the whole thing together. Each individual component is measured and built specifically for its own unique location. Each part is numbered to allow correct reassembly. It can be seen that the whole interlocking structure made a great contribution to the rigidity of the whole ship. On the floor of the hold were the "buikdenning" (floor-boards). The ship's bottom beneath the buikdenning was kept oiled with a mixture of old engine oil, linseed oil and tar. The buikdenning themselves were oiled or tarred on the bottom side, but mostly left natural, or coated with boiled linseed oil on the upper side. On a modern conversion, the steel coach-roof without the addition of substantial gebinten, must take the place of all these combining elements. This must be born in mind when converting or buying a ready made conversion. A skutsje, for example, might originally have had a den of 15cm in height; even a large zeilkast only had a 75 cm high den. Many conversions routinely raise this to 1 metre or more, and in addition may incorporate several very large panoramic windows. If done well this is not a problem, but lightly built, cheap options, should be recognized for what they are.

62) *"Volharding"*, built to carry rolls of paper, has slightly curved metal hatch-boards. Fastening is by a variation of the hasp and eye.

63) The modern Belgian motor-ship *"Pro Deo"* shows her one-piece, sliding, aluminium hatch-covers.

64)
a)Teboekstellingnummer

b) Metingsmerk

c) IJkmerk

Registration & Measurement

From the beginning of this century, in common with many industrial activities, barge trade started to become heavily regulated. For the latter day owner or researcher this is actually a blessing, as it means that numerous records were kept of ships and their owners. Crucially, the ships were required to be measured, registered and marked accordingly.

MEETBRIEF

The "meetbrief" is the registration book belonging to an individual vessel. Each ship was given a unique number on initial registration and this number, which is also the "meetbrief nummer" stayed with the ship for life. On older ships, the date of initial registration as given in the meetbrief is not necessarily the same as the launching date. Certainly many ships trading in the latter part of the nineteenth century were not registered on the "modern" system until the early part of this century, in the 1920's.

For registration purposes, the 11 provinces making up the Netherlands at the beginning of this century were split into three "metingsdistricts".

Rotterdam: signified by the letter **R**, covered the provinces of Limburg, Noord Brabant, Zeeland and that part of Zuid-Holland below a line joining the cities of Leiden and Utrecht.

Amsterdam: signified by the letter **A**, covered the areas of Zuid-Holland above a line joining the cities of Leiden and Utrecht, and the provinces of Noord-Holland, Utrecht and Gelderland.

Groningen: signified by the letter **G**, covered the provinces of Groningen, Friesland, Drente and Overijssel.

A vessel that had permanent residence, or intended to trade in any of these areas, was measured and registered by the "ijkkantoor", the local weights and measures department. In each of the three metingsdistricts there were many separate "kadasters" (registration offices) situated in the main towns of the region. These offices would handle the three separate registration and measuring procedures.

1) IJKMERK
2) TEBOEKSTELLINGNUMMER
3) METINGSMERK

IJkmerk

The "ijker" was the official weights and measures officer who was responsible for calculating the acceptable loading capacity of a ship trading in a pre-defined area. When the calculations were complete he issued a number, the "ijkmerk", which was stamped into the ship's side. The location of this number is detailed very precisely in the meetbrief (paragraph 28); it appears twice on each side of the ship at bow and stern. A horizontal line drawn between the two numbers corresponds with the maximum loaded waterline in fresh water.

Every time a ship moved into a different trading area it was required to be re-measured. The maximum allowable waterline in sheltered canals was markedly different to that deemed safe in exposed or open waters. My ship has three different sets of ijkmerken. The first issued in s'Gravenhage (Den Haag), in 1901, has the relatively low number of 168. The next two numbers, issued in Amsterdam in 1934 and 1944 respectively, have more digits: being 8517 and 12646. The more recent the measurement, the longer the number. When a ship was re-measured and a new ijkmerk issued, the old numbers were striped through with a chisel. The "old" 1934 ijkmerk is 23 cm lower than the "new" one issued in 1944, which allows the waterline to reach side-deck level.

Teboekstellingnummer

When the measuring and marking was complete, the kadaster would issue another unique number, signifying when and where the registration was done. This number, the "teboekstellingnummer", is in four parts.

210 B AMST 1927

This is the current teboekstellingnummer on my own ship. The numbers simply mean that it was the 210th ship registered in that year. The B is very important. It means Binnenvaart, or inland trade (a ship trading on coastal routes or in the Baltic for example had to be strongly built to a higher specification and these ships would have a Z for Zeevaart as part of their teboekstellingnummer). AMST of course means the registration office was in Amsterdam. These letters generally take the form of the first four or so letters of the town in question. ZWOL for Zwolle, APPING for Appingedam, DEV for Deventer, LEID for Leiden, UTR for Utrecht, ARNH for Arnhem, etc. etc. The last four numbers signify the year the number was issued.

The location of the teboekstellingnummer is given in the meetbrief (paragraph 69).

Metingsmerk

After measurement the meetbrief was issued. At the same time a number was assigned to the vessel. This became the meetbriefnummer and also the ship's number ("metingsmerk" or "brandmerk"). It consisted of the signifying letter of the area, the letter "N" denoting Netherlands and a unique number. In my own Amsterdam registered ship this is A N 31. This number appeared in the form of a brass plate riveted to the ship's side. However time showed that these plates tended to drop off due to wear and tear and later ships had the number stamped into the fabric of the hull and also into the superstructure. The location of the number is given in the meetbrief (paragraph 31). This is mostly in the area of the cockpit or wheel-house. On my paviljoentjalk *"Jan Willem"*, it is on the forward centre edge of the paviljoendek. On the luxemotor *"Vertrouwen"*, I found it on the forward facing edge of the salonroef on the starboard side.

Officially, the registration office had to be notified of any change of trading area, change of ownership, change of name of ship, or any substantial alteration to the ship such as lengthening, conversion to motor, or change of existing motor. The ship could then be re-measured if appropriate and the meetbrief altered accordingly. Every change in the meetbrief, which in any case had to be renewed every fifteen years, cost hard earned money. The more prosperous skippers and those owners with large fleets tended to be scrupulous about such things, but the thousands of one-ship-skippers couldn't afford to be so precise, unfortunately leading to gaps in documentation and problems for the researcher. However, if you are able to locate the metingsnummer, or better still a teboekstellingnummer, by contacting the "scheepskadaster" in the relevant town, it is often possible to unearth more of the history of your ship.

Happy Hunting!

65) *"Egbert"*

Glossary

A

Aak	ship type, or generally used for any "barge".
Aanvaringsklamp	heavy wooden block, fixed to the hull in front of the lee-board to protect it from collision.
Achteronder	living or storage space under the aft deck.
Achterschip	the aft end of the ship.
Achtersteven	sternpost.
Anderhalfmast	ketch rigged ship with short mizzen mast.
Anker	anchor.
Ankerlier	anchor winch.

B

Bakboord	port (side).
Bakstag	backstay.
Bakstagtakel	tackle for running backstay.
Balland	type of Belgian motor-barge.
Bedrijfsvaartuig	commercial (as opposed to pleasure) ship.
Beltvaarder	ship trading in the Belt area of the Baltic.
Benzine	petrol.
Beretand	wooden posts on either side of the voorsteven on sailing-ships (literally bear's teeth).
Berghout	rubbing strake.
Bergplaat	area of hull plate covered by the berghout.
Beugel	cotton or canvas bucket on long pole used when dredging.
Beurtschip	ship providing a regular local service, commonly used as the name for a small motor-ship type.
Bezaan	mizzen mast, after mast on a ketch rigged ship.
Binnenvaart	inland shipping trade.
Binnenschip	inland trade ship.
Binten	(also gebinten) athwartship metal beams tying the sides of the hold together.
Boegspriet	bowsprit.
Boegstag	whisker stay for bowsprit.
Boeisel	area of the ship's side above the berghout.
Bokkepoot	"A' frame used for mast lowering (literally goats leg, also a type of biscuit).
Bol	ball or sphere (literally) also a sailing-barge type.
Bolder	bollard.
Bollestal	north Netherlands word for steering position or cockpit.
Boltjalk	north Netherlands ship type.
Botteloef	fabricated extension on voorsteven of a sailing-ship to allow a larger fore-triangle.
Bouwjaar	year of building.

B

Bouwmateriaal	building material.
Bovenhout	ultra short gaff (see driekant).
Braadspil	spike and barrel type manual windlass.
Brandmerken	official registration number stamped into the ship's structure.
Breefok	square sail carried on a yard.
Buikdenning	boards forming the floor of the hold.

C

Chartervaart	charter trade.
Composietschip	ship built from a combination of metal and wood.

D

Dekhuis	small living space on deck.
Deklast	cargo carried on deck above the level of the hatch-boards.
Den	the vertical sides of the hold above the side-decks.
Dirk	tackle that allows the gaff or boom to be used as a crane (English "derrick").
Doornikker	barge built for trade in the Doornik area.
Doossteven	fabricated, square section, hollow stem or sternpost, found on most iron and steel barges.
Dortmunder	large German motor-barge.
Driekant	three sided sail carried on an ultra short gaff .
Dwarsscheeps	athwartships.

E

Ebbe	ebb tide.
Echte	genuine.
Eigenaar	owner.

F

Ferrytuig	spritsail rig.
Fok	foresail closest to the mainmast.
Fokschoot	sheet for the fok.
Fokval	halyard for the fok.
Friesetjalk	regional ship type (Friesland).

G

Gaffel	gaff.
Gang	hull plate in iron or steel ship.
Gangboord	side-deck.
Gasolie	diesel fuel.
Geklonken	riveted.
Giek	boom.
Groningertjalk	regional ship type (Groningen).
Grootzeil	mainsail.
Groteschoot	mainsheet.

H

Hagenaar	ship built to trade in the city of Den Haag.
Halfwinder	large down-wind foresail.
Hanepoot	metal band on the upper part of the mast to which the shrouds are fastened.
Hekschroef	conventionally fitted propeller.
Hektjalk	type of tjalk with distinctive high stern.
Helmhout	shaped wooden tiller.
Helmstok	tiller.
Herna	type of Belgian built barge.
Heve	Part of the hull where the keel plates curve upwards at bow and stern.
Hijstuigen	mast, boom and lifting tackle used for loading cargo.
Holte	general use; hold or cargo space. precise use; the vertical distance between the underside of the side-deck at its lowest point and the top-side of the keel plate.
Hommer	part of the mast at which the Hanepoot is located, or the shroud made fast to.
Hondsvoet	part of a block around which the tail of the sheet is made fast.
Hulptuig	small mast and sailing-rig used on early motor-barges.

I

IJkmerk	number issued by weights and measures office.
IJzer	iron.
Inzinking	displacement.

J

Jaaglijn	line used to tow a barge from the shore.
Jaagmast	mast to which a jaaglijn is attached.
Jufferblok	"deadeye" used to tension rigging.

K

Kadaster	registry office.
Kajuit	cabin.
Kast	type of Dutch built barge.
Kattalie	system used to trice the mainsail on a sailing-barge.
Kattespoor	bottom frame.
Katwijker	barge built to specific dimensions for use in the town of Katwijk.
Kempenaar	barge built originally for use on the Kemperkanaal.
Kielplaat	the central plate on the bottom of a barge.
Kim	turn of the bilge.
Kisten	small area in the fore-part of a barge containing chain, ropes etc.
Klik	ornament found on after end of tiller.
Klinknagel	rivet.
Klipper	sailing-barge type.
Klipperaak	as above but with an aak stern.
Kluiver	sail set in front of fok.
Kluiverboom	bowsprit.

K

Knecht	deck-hand, also pinrail at the foot of the mast.
Knie	knee, structural hull member.
Knuttel	reef point.
Koekoek	skylight.
Koftjalk	type of seagoing tjalk.
Kokerluik	hatch in fore-deck allowing keel-stepped mast to pivot upwards.
Kolsum	structural part of ship on which the mast is stepped.
Kont	stern of ship (literally, arse).
Kop	bow of ship (literally, head).
Koppelverband	system coupling two ships stem to stern.
Koproer	lowering rudder found in the forepart of some barges.
Kopschroef	bow propeller.
Kraak	type of sailing-barge.
Kraanlijn	topping lift.
Kromsteven	any ship with a curved stempost.
Kruiphoogte	air draft of loaded ship (literaly "crawl height").
Kruiserhek	type of stern found on larger motor-barges.
Kustvaart	coastal trade.

L

Lamme arm	side mounted propeller (see zijschroef).
Lier	winch.
Lijnolie	linseed oil.
Loefbijter	below water protrusion on stempost of some sailing-barges.
Luik	hatch.
Lummel	fitting at base of mast to which the boom is connected.
Luxemotor	type of motor-barge.

M

Mastdek	see Kolsum.
Mastkoker	fitting on deck securing base of mast (tabernacle).
Mastwortel	carved spiral ornament at the top of the mast.
Meetbrief	official registration book.
Merkel	athwartships beam supporting the hatch-boards.
Metingsmerk	official registration number.
Mignole	type of "spits-like" motor-barge.
Mixte	ship built from both wood and metal (see compositieschip).
Motorhek	type of stern often found on motor-barges used in shallow waters.

N

Nagelbank	(see knecht).
Nok	peak of gaff.

O

Opdrukker	(see below).
Opduwer	small motor-boat pushing a larger engineless barge.
Opsteker	adjustable extension to botteloef.
Overloop	traveller for fok or grootzeil.

P

Paardenroef	on-board stable for horse or mule.
Pakschuit	cargo or passenger barge designed to be pulled from the shore.
Paviljoen	after-cabin.
Paviljoentjalk	tjalk with an after-cabin.
Peniche	type of French built motor-barge.
Platbodem	flat bottom.
Poon	type of tjalk originating in Zeeland.
Potdeksel	bulwark.
Praam	sailing-barge type.
Punter	open flat-bottomed ship's boat, usually rowed or sculled.

R

Raderboot	paddle-wheel tugboat.
Rakband	lacings holding the sail to the mast.
Rietaak	aak type from the Biesbos area.
Roef	cabin having windows above deck-level.
Roer	rudder.
Roerlichter	device used to prevent the rudder swinging when not in use.
Roerzwaard	lowering rudder extension.
Romp	hull.

S

Salonroef	roef located after the steering position.
Scheepsjager	person who made a living from towing barges from the shore.
Scheerbalk	central spine locating the hatch-boards.
Scheg	skeg
Schildpadkatrol	particular variety of block.
Schoener	large sailing-barge type.
Schouw	small flat-bottomed boat with a hard chine.
Skutsje	type of tjalk found in Friesland.
Sleepboot	tugboat.
Sleepschip	dumb barge, designed to be towed by a tugboat.
Sluis	lock.
Snik	type of barge designed to be towed from the shore.
Sontvaarder	ship trading in the Sont area of the Baltic.
Spant	structural frames.
Spiegel	coloured area on the stern of many sailing-barges (literally, mirror).
Spijker	nail.
Spits	type of motor-barge.
Spitsbek	variation of above.
Stag	stay (as in forestay).
Steilsteven	ship with a straight stempost, also particular sailing-barge type.
Strijkklamp	timber against which the lee-board lies.
Stuiten	thick area of the rubbing strake at bow and stern.
Stuurboord	starboard.
Stuurstand	open steering position.
Stuurtalie	restraining device on tiller.

T

Takel	tackle.
Talie	line used in conjunction with a block.
Teboekstelling- -nummer	unique number issued in the area in which the ship is trading.
Theehut	small cabin found behind the wheel-house on Belgian built barges.
Tjalk	sailing-barge type.
Tonnetje	handgrip in the shape of a barrel located on the end of the tiller.
Top	area of the mast above the hommer.
Treklijn	see jaaglijn.
Tuigage	sailing-rigging.

U

Uitwip	see kokerluik.

V

Vaarboom	pole used to push the barge along from on deck.
Val	halyard (as in fokval).
Vioolblok	violin shaped double block.
Vlak	flat area of a ship's bottom.
Vlet	small flat-bottomed sailing boat.
Vleugel	masthead flag.
Vooronder	fore-cabin.
Voorsteven	stempost.

W

Wadvaarder	ship trading in the Wad area of the Baltic.
Walenschip	type of Belgian built barge.
Want	shroud.
Waterstag	lower stay on bowsprit.
Weeflijn	rope attached to the shrouds to form a ladder (ratlines).
Wegerij	counterweight on the foot of the mast.
Wellingplaat	area of the ships side behind the berghout.
Westlander	type of small barge originating in the Westland area of the Netherlands.
Wimple	see vleugel.
Woonboot	houseboat (static).
Woonschip	houseboat (mobile).

Z

Zandaak	aak type barge designed for the dredging and carriage of sand.
Zandloper	metal reinforcing piece on the leading edge of a lee-board.
Zeebrief	official document allowing a ship to trade on the sea.
Zeeg	"sheer" of the ship's hull.
Zeezwaard	long and thin lee-board designed for use at sea.
Zeilroef	cabin located forward of the steering position.
Zetboord	wooden board carrying the ship's name, owner's name and home port.
Zijschroef	side mounted propeller, driven from an engine forward of the mast.
Zwaard	lee-board.
Zwaardloper	tackle for raising and lowering the lee-board.
Zwanehals	swan-neck connection joining the boom to the lummel.

BIBLIOGRAPHY

Coltrane, R & Binias, J. *Coltranes Planes & Automobiles*, Simon & Schuster, 1997.

Dessens, H. *De Hazenbergen modellen*, De Boer Maritiem, 1991.

Dessens, H, et al. *Scheepsrestauratie*, De Boer Maritiem, 1988.

Dutch Barge Association. *The Barge Buyers Handbook*, DBA, 1998.

Frederiks, G. *De Ideaal*. Ploegsma, 1980.

Groenwagen, G. *Hollandse Schepen*, van den Brink, 1789.

Groot, H de. *Volaan Vooruit*, De Alk, 1989.

Groot, H de & Biezenaar J. *Rijn en Binnenvaart in Beeld*, De Alk, 1991.

Hin, F, et al. *Scheepstypologieen*, De Boer Maritiem, 1980.

Joode, T de & Bernard, P. *De Mens en Het Water*, Uitgeverij M&P bv, undated.

Klimbie, B. *De Vrachtvaarders van Europa*, De Alk 1987.

Kooiman, J. *Varen Met Platbodems*, De Boer Maritiem, 1987.

Leather, J. *Barges*, Adlard Coles, 1984.

Loomeijer, F and Martin, R. *Binnenvaart Schepen*, De Alk, 1977.

Loomeijer, F. *Met Zeil en Treil*, De Alk, 1980.

Loomeijer, F. *Zeilende Kustvaarders*, De Alk, 1985.

LVZB, *Schepenlijst* 1991.

Marten, R and Westra, L. *Glorie van de Oude Binnenvaart*, and *Weerzien Met De Oude Binnenvaart*, Uitgeversmaatschappij Amsterdam (undated).

Menzel, H. *Die Tjalk*, Alte Schiffe Verlag, 1993.

Oostrom, C. *Ronde en Platbodems*, De Alk, 1988.

Schenk, P. *Operation Sealion*, Conway Maritime, 1990.

Speerstra, H. *De Laatste Echte Schippers*, De Boer Maritiem, 1976.

The journals of :

The Dutch Barge Association, c/o Carl Waters, "De Hoop", Ryepeck Meadow, Chertsy Road, Shepperton, Middlesex, TW17 9NU.

The Barge Cruising Association, c/o John Griffin, Bossington Wharf, Rothschild Road, Linslade, Leighton Buzzard, Bedfordshire, LU7 7TF.

LVBZB, postbus 2004, 100 CA Amsterdam, The Netherlands.

Special thanks to **Han Visser** for all his help, to **Rob Martens** for the loan of his original photographs, to **Uitgeverij De Alk** for allowing me to reproduce many archive pictures and most important of all, special thanks to my wife **Margreet**, without whose patience and editing skills this book would never have been finished.

Illustration sources

a) *Rijn en Binnenvaart in Beeld.*
b) *Weerzien met de Oude Binnenvaart.*
c) *Glorie van de Oude Binnenvaart.*
d) Author.
Others as given below.

Illustration No

1)	d	34)	..
2)	..	35)	..
3)	..	36)	..
4)	..	37)	c
5)	..	38)	a
6)	..	39)	..
7)	..	40)	d
8)	..	41)	b
9)	..	42)	..
10)	..	43)	a
11)	..	44)	Rob Martens
12)	..	45)	a
13)	c	46)	Bokkepoot
14)	a	47)	b
15)	d	48)	a
16)	..	49)	..
17)	..	50)	d
18)	..	51)	a
19)	a	52)	Schepenlijst
20)	d	53)	..
21)	a	54)	Bundesarchiv
22)	Schepenlijst	55)	..
23)	..	56)	d
24)	..	57)	..
25)	a	58)	..
26)	..	59)	Bokkepoot
27)	c	60)	d
28)	..	61)	..
29)	a	62)	..
30)	b	63)	..
31)	Bokkepoot	64)	..
32)	a	65)	..
33)	..		